The Logic of Scientific Inference
An Introduction

The Logic of Scientific Inference

An Introduction

Jennifer Trusted

Foreword
Sir Peter Medawar

First published 1979 by
THE MACMILLAN PRESS LTD
London and Basingstoke
Associated companies in Delhi Dublin
Hong Kong Johannesburg Lagos Melbourne
New York Singapore and Tokyo

Photoset, printed and bound
in Great Britain by
REDWOOD BURN LIMITED
Trowbridge & Esher

British Library Cataloguing in Publication Data

Trusted, Jennifer
   The logic of scientific inference. – (Modern
introductions to philosophy).
   1.   Induction (Logic)
   I. Title II. Series
   161   BC91

ISBN 0-333-26669-2
ISBN 0-333-26670-6 Pbk

To my Father

Contents

Foreword

For more than three hundred years informed opinion about scientific method has been dominated by the thought of one intellectual giant or another – a Bacon, Hume, Kant, Whewell, Mill, or Popper – men who have argued so persuasively with such intellectual strength that people have willingly fallen into step with their way of thinking. Dr Trusted is respectful about them all but not in the least overawed and thank goodness there is no sign in her of that maverick tendency we have latterly found among young methodologists who seem wholly preoccupied by liberating themselves from the opinions of their teachers. No. This is a book *sui generis* and the great thing about it is its freshness – of intellectual approach, and of examples taken from both natural and unnatural sciences. She has no uneasiness about seeming sometimes to be old-fashioned: thus she is at one with Mill in insisting that induction is an ampliative process. Mill was very firm about this: writing of induction he said:

> Any process in which what seems the conclusion is no greater than the premises from which it is drawn, does not fall within the meaning of the term.

I have been coming with increasing conviction to think that Popper's notion of an *a priori* 'expectation of order' is one of the most illuminating ideas in methodology. Dr Trusted's remarks on the subject (p.62) are sensible and clarifying.

It is another example of freshness of Jennifer Trusted's approach that the story she tells has a happy ending. Inductive and hypothetico-deductive schemes of thought are reconciled she believes by the consideration that devising an explanatory hypothesis itself involves an inductive process, even though this may perhaps be 'a matter for psychologists rather than for philosophers'.

Philosophers of science, like philosophers generally, never *wholly* agree with each other and I do not agree with everything that Dr Trusted says, but I agree with so much of it and approve so warmly of the general spirit of her text that I very much hope it reaches a wider audience than that which she modestly hopes for, viz: philosophers and philosophers of science and maybe some scientists too.

The reason why I hope for a wider audience is because of the almost universally held belief that scientists practise something that is thought of as 'the' scientific method, as if they had at their command some formulary of reasoning or calculus of discovery that empowered them to arrive with certainty at the truth.

Scientists would be beggared in next to no time if any such view prevailed widely. If it were true, what excuse could we scientists give for not solving a scientific problem if it were our professional business to do so? There are some medical scientists whose business it is to find out why people get rheumatoid arthritis and how they may be cured of it. Why then don't they do so? If there were indeed such a thing as '*the* scientific method' it could only be because they are either ignorant of it or too lazy to carry it out. It follows that if there were any such thing as *the* scientific method, nearly all scientists should be sacked.

Knowing as I do from experience what strange and unsystematic contrivances of mind, of unreasonable expectations and wounds of ideas falsified go into making a scientific theory, I sometimes wonder thàt science goes forward at all. I share Jennifer Trusted's hope that scientists will find this book interesting and believe also that they will find it a help.

P. B. Medawar
February, 1979.

Preface

The purpose of this book is to give a simple account of some aspects of scientific reasoning. It is primarily a text-book for those who wish to study philosophy, and history and philosophy of science, but I hope it may also be interesting to and useful for scientists. Because it is designed as a textbook, there are at the end, and related to each chapter, some questions to test understanding, together with suggestions for further reading.

The view taken is that induction, or ampliative inference, is essential for knowledge of the world which we know from sense perception. That is to say, our common-sense knowledge and our more sophisticated scientific knowledge are arrived at by a process which must involve induction, although knowledge is not and cannot be acquired by that alone.

The relation between induction and analogy is considered in order to bring out their interdependence. The role of observation and experimentation is discussed, and then the problem of justifying the reliability of inductive inference from observation and experiment is considered. The importance is stressed of the relation of theories to simple particular facts, to generalisations and to scientific laws. There is also discussion of the notion of causality and the establishment of empirical causal connections. Finally there is a very elementary and non-mathematical account of probability as it applies to universal and to statistical generalisations.

It is assumed that readers have not studied logic or philosophy; and, though most of the examples are taken from the physical sciences, no special scientific or mathematical knowledge is required to understand the argument.

Acknowledgement

I should like to thank Professor Daniel O'Connor for his help and encouragement in the writing of this book. I have also had some valuable advice from many friends. I should particularly like to thank Professor Sir Alfred Ayer, Professor Peter Gray F.R.S. and Dr David Knight for sympathetic and constructive criticism. Any mistakes in the text are, of course, my own.

J. T.

The Nature of Induction

(i) Induction as a Form of Ampliative Inference

Induction is a particular kind of inference. To infer, or to make an inference, is to derive a conclusion from some given premises by some process which is accepted as a rational one. The classical form of inference is *deductive* inference. Here the process of inference is in accordance with accepted rules of logic, and, if the inference is valid, that is, if the rules are correctly followed, the conclusion cannot be false if the premises are true, since the conclusion can contain no *more* information than is found in the premises. Consider:

	All men are mortal	– major premise
	Socrates is a man	– minor premise
Therefore	Socrates is mortal	– conclusion

Knowing that all men are mortal and that Socrates is a man, we already have the information that Socrates is mortal in the premises.

Not all deductive arguments are as simple as this, and deductive inferences such as those made in geometry, and in mathematics generally, are of immense value in that they reveal and make explicit that which lies in the premises. For a sufficiently powerful mind most of the theorems of arithmetic* and geometry would follow as obvious

* It has been shown that it is not possible for all true arithmetical propositions to be logically deduced from any given set of axioms – see Nagel and Newman, *Gödel's Proof*, in the reading list for this chapter.

conclusions from the premises or axioms of arithmetic and geometry; but since human minds are not so powerful, deduction, a process which may be long and arduous, is invaluable in helping to show the implications of the axioms. However, the fact remains that deductive inference can never tell us *more* than is contained in the axioms, and, since the axioms are devised by us, deductive inference can only reveal the nature of our own constructed systems.

There is, however, another form of inference – ampliative inference – whereby conclusions obtained contain *more* information than is contained in the premises. Here the reasoning leads from premises which can be taken as known by direct experience to conclusions which are unknown – that is, which have not been observed or experienced. The inference may be from descriptions of particular observed events to predictions (or retrodictions) of further particular events in the future (or in the past). But very often, especially in science, the inference is from descriptions of particular observed events to a generalisation about an indefinitely large number of similar but not observed particulars which may be in the past, present or future. It is convenient to distinguish inference from known to unknown particulars, and inference from known particulars to generalisations. The first form of inference may be called *eduction*; the second form of inference may be called *induction*. They are both forms of ampliative inference. Here we are primarily concerned with induction.

(ii) Induction Basic to Learning and to Perception

The ability to generalise from particular experiences is natural and spontaneous. As young children we observe that the white crystals called sugar taste sweet, and quite spontaneously we make the generalisation that all such crystals taste sweet. We observe that most objects will fall to the ground from our perambulators and we take it for granted that any objects will fall. Later these early generalisations may need to be qualified, but in early life we spontaneously make hundreds of such generalisations and we are held to be *learning* about the world around us. This world around us is called the *empirical world*; it is the world which we can only start to learn about by means of our senses: sight, sound, touch, smell and taste. The empirical world may therefore also be called the *world of sense*.

When we say that we learn about the empirical world from past experience, we are in fact saying that on account of past experiences we are able to make generalisations which help us to interpret present experience and which guide our behaviour. So induction is the means whereby we learn from past experience, for, unless we could make generalisations on the *basis* of past experience, past experience would be of no use to us. Science grows from common-sense knowledge of the world; scientific generalisations grow from the spontaneously made generalisations of everyday life. Induction is fundamental to our ability to learn from experience and is fundamental to our acquiring scientific knowledge as well as common-sense knowledge.

But induction is even more fundamental than this. It is not only the means whereby we learn from experience, it is the means whereby we have any conscious experience at all. As already stated, our experience of the empirical world must arise from our sensations, but sensations alone are not enough. Sensations must be interpreted if they are to give us knowledge. At best a pure sensation can only tell us something about ourselves, not about the empirical world around us. Sensations are the basis, but no more than the basis, of what is called *sense-perception*, through which bare sensations are recognised, compared and classified so that they can be interpreted.

A question arises at once. How can this process of recognition and classification begin? After all, the very first sensation we receive could only be recognised if we were equipped with some inborn or innate knowledge of what is in the world, and it is unlikely that this is so. Aristotle considered the problem of how sensations came to be recognised and classified: the problem of how sense-perception was possible. He described the beginning of our recognition of similarities in the hurly-burly of sensations as being like the stand which might be made by one man when all around him are in flight in a battle. When one man makes a stand, then others stand by him and so the disorderly rout may be stopped and a line of battle may be formed. Similarly, the muddle of undiscriminated sensations may become orderly perceptions when one particular sensation 'makes a stand', that is, is understood to be like another.

Today the problem remains a problem in psychology and is one which perhaps may be solved with the help of experiments with animals, as well as human beings. It is suggested that our very first sensations make some sort of imprint in the brain. Experiments with animals indicate that this may be so, and that such imprints may firmly fix the animal's response to its surroundings. In man, imprints, if they occur, seem to be modified more easily, though it is well known that early impressions can have a powerful effect on character and personality. However the *means* whereby we first arrive at conscious experience are no longer a problem for philosophers. Rather it is important for philosophers to appreciate that our early and most simple conscious experiences are already ordered. Expectation of order, the expectation that it will be possible to recognise and classify sensations, is innate in us and in many animals. We do not have to be taught to perceive; we spontaneously make the generalisations – that is, the inductions – by which our sensations are interpreted.

This spontaneous induction is absolutely essential; it is the basis of experience just as much as sensations themselves. It is only because we can carry out such spontaneous inductions that we have experience, and therefore it is only because we can carry out inductions that we can even begin to have knowledge of the empirical world. Induction is used in forming the simple concepts of phenomena of the everyday world. This process is analogous to the way induction helps us to form the sophisticated concepts of the entities postulated by scientific theories (see chapter 5, section i).

When the baby is able to recognise his mother he shows he possesses a concept of his mother – indeed if we take it that possession of a concept is possession of a capacity, we may say that possession of a simple concept *is* the capacity to recognise.

When the baby has formed a concept of his mother he has already started the process of generalising whereby he has present expectation, for example, of what his mother is like and whereby he can anticipate the future – in other words he anticipates what his mother will do. Because he has certain expectations, certain sensations are expected and most readily recognised. Unexpected sensations are less likely to be recognised; they are likely to be disregarded unless they are intense, in which case they may be recognised with distaste or even fear. In other words, because we have expectations our minds are not equally receptive to all stimuli from the empirical world. They are not like pieces of blank paper, ready to be written on, or like pieces of soft wax, ready to receive all impressions equally well. Our minds actively sort and classify sensations; they can be compared to searchlights, directed to and illuminating those parts of the world which they find particularly interesting.

(iii) Correction of Spontaneous Induction by Scientific Induction

We have to admit that on the most simple level, a level little different from that attained by many animals, we are involved in the sorting and classifying of sensations, and in discriminating amongst available stimuli. Primitive as this capacity is, it is the basis of all our knowledge of the world. Where we differ from animals is in carrying out inductions at a conscious level also; this may lead us to modify our original spontaneous inductions.

The dog recognises his master and the baby his mother. The dog, like the baby, learns that certain things are pleasant to eat and *acts* as though he has made a generalisation which guides his behaviour. So does the baby. Adult man may modify his earlier generalisations since he has acquired far more knowledge of the world than either the baby or animals. This is not because his senses are more acute – in many cases they are much less acute – but because he has consciously elaborated the natural process of spontaneous induction.

It is the purpose of this book to study the uses and limitations of these more sophisticated inductions, that is, to see *how* they help to give us knowledge and also how this knowledge may be criticised. The generalisations which we make about the empirical world cannot be rigidly classified, but there are three virtually different types of generalisation:

(1) spontaneous inductions
(2) inductions arrived at by reflective common sense
(3) inductions arrived at through critical scientific study.

Recognition of simple objects such as tables and chairs, materials such as water, salt and sugar, and people such as our parents, is the result of spontaneous induction, the capacity we have in common with animals. It is usually described as the capacity of arriving at simple concepts. Recognition of the sun as fire in the sky and anticipation of its rising tomorrow, anticipation of the cold of winter and the warmth of summer all arise from common-sense induction. Such inductions are not as fundamental as the former group in that they require some reflection, probably more than most animals are capable of, but they do not require much intellectual deliberation. Lastly there are scientific inductions such as those whereby eclipses and hurricanes may be predicted, the behaviour of chemical elements and compounds described, and the various generalisations and laws which are taught in schools and universities, and which have been confirmed by carefully designed experiments or directed observations. Scientific inductions may be generalisations about phenomena which can be directly observed, but they may also be generalisations about theoretical entities which are not directly observable. For example, 'The pressure of a gas is inversely proportional to its volume at constant temperature' is a scientific induction; the generalisation 'Atoms of a particular element have the same electronic structure' is also a scientific induction.

As was indicated above, many spontaneous generalisations of type (1) may come to be modified and elaborated in the light of more sophisticated thought. It is even more common that the generalisations of reflective common sense, type (2), may be modified or even rejected. It is for instance a common-sense generalisation that the sun goes round the earth; it is a common-sense generalisation that the earth is flat; both these generalisations are rejected by more careful deliberation.

Thus, although induction is fundamental to knowledge of the empirical world, it is not the case that the primitive inductions are *necessarily* the ones which give us the most secure knowledge. Further experience and thought may lead us to modify generalisations which at one time had been thought true beyond question. One example is the modification we have made of the fundamental common-sense generalisation that the sun goes round the earth. There is relative motion, but this is better regarded as a consequence of the earth travelling round the sun. A more recent modification is the result of Einstein's Relativity Theory. We have had to modify our generalisations about the nature of space; we no longer consider it to be the space postulated by Euclidean geometry.

We can never be absolutely sure that we *have* empirical knowledge, for the basis of all such knowledge, the inductive generalisations, cannot be *proved* to be immune from revision in the light of further experience. There is always the possibility that more information (more experience) and/or more careful thought, may lead us to modify our scientific generalisations so as to make changes in more basic generalisations. Such insecurity must be accepted, and it is necessary to allow for the imperfections or possible imperfections in our empirical knowledge. Induction cannot be shown to be immune from error.

Inductive inferences cannot be shown to lead to conclusions which are certainly true, even though all the premises, that is the descriptions of the particular events, are true. Inductive inferences therefore differ in an important way from deductive inferences. But we must make the best of what we have, for inductive inference is the process by which we acquire knowledge from sense. Inductions support all our knowledge of the empirical world (see also chapter 5, section ii, and for Questions and Further Reading related to this chapter see p. 136).

2

Analogy

(i) Argument from Analogy

Analogy means likeness. If two or more objects or two or more events show analogy, then there is some likeness between them, that is they have some property or properties in common. For example, there is analogy between an orange and the sun in that both are round and may have an orange colour; there is analogy between a fire and the sun in that both give out heat; there is analogy between the earth and all the planets in that they all move round the sun in elliptical orbits; there is analogy between an eclipse of the moon and an eclipse of the sun, in that both involve the temporary disappearance of a heavenly body from our sight. It is possible to think of analogies between almost any pair of objects. Some analogies may appear trivial, like the analogy between the sun and an orange, and some may appear important like the analogy between the earth and the planets; but in fact whether or not the analogy is trivial will depend on what our argument is about. Thus the analogy between the sun and an orange is irrelevant and trivial if we are concerned with the possibility of a limit to the age of the sun, but if we were concerned with the shape of the sun, and its apparent complete disappearance in an eclipse, the analogy with an orange might be helpful. Similarly the analogy between the earth and the planets would seem irrelevant if we were considering whether there was life on the planets, but if we were considering the question of the origin of the solar system, this likeness between the earth and the planets would be important. Again, the analogy between man and the beetle, in that both are living creatures, appears irrelevant if we are considering the habitat of beetles, but, if we are considering death from radioactive emanation it would be important.

As a general rule we may say that if two or more things are alike in some respect, that is, if they show analogy, there is a tendency to expect likeness in other respects. As mentioned above, there is almost always some analogy between any pair of objects, so that we may say that there is a general tendency to expect likeness. Moreover, if there is apparent extensive likeness, that is, if the analogy is extended or close, we are more likely to consider that there are yet further likenesses. An argument which suggests that, because there is likeness in some respect between two or more things, there may be yet further likeness, is called an argument from analogy. The more resemblances that can be established, the stronger becomes the argument that there shall be yet further likeness, that is, the stronger is the argument from analogy. For example, we do not think the argument that because a certain leaf is nourishing for beetles it will be a good food for man is very strong, even though both man and beetle are animals. Indeed we should not be at all surprised if the leaves were poisonous for man. This is because the analogy between man and beetle is not very close. There is closer analogy between man and the horse in that both are mammals, and if the leaves were found to nourish horses, we should be more inclined to believe that they would be food for man. Because there is even closer analogy between men and monkeys in that both are primates we should be much more confident in the nourishing power of leaves which were food for monkeys. Lastly, if we knew that a particular group of men, or even one man, had found such leaves nourishing we should be practically certain that they were a nourishing food. This may seem an example rather unlikely to be used in practice, but it is not far removed from examples in medical science. A new drug may first be tried on mice or rats, then on monkeys, and finally on some patient who does not respond to more orthodox treatment. It does not require many such tests on particular individuals to be successful, for it to be assumed that the drug can be generally used. Sometimes, as in the case of the thalidomide tragedy, it turns out that we have been too hasty and that the assumption is not correct; but the vast majority of tested drugs are beneficial when used in the appropriate circumstances. In the early stages particular individuals receive the drug, and the case for the drugs being considered safe for everyone rests on arguments from analogy. The closer the analogy between the test cases and others, the greater is the confidence we have in the drug.

In general we may say that the closer the established analogy, the greater is the confidence that there is yet further analogy, and the stronger is the argument from analogy.

On reflection it may seem strange that if considerable resemblance has already been observed, we should expect yet further resemblance. If properties of objects were distributed at random it would seem that, if two or more subjects had been shown to resemble each other in some respect there would be no particular reason for them being alike in other respects, and if more resemblance was found, this would not increase the likelihood of yet further resemblance. But the world does not seem to be like this; it is a fact of our experience that certain groups of properties are regularly associated, and if two or more objects exhibit certain properties in common, experience shows us that it is likely that they will have other properties in common. The more resemblance which can be established, the more likely it is that the objects will share yet more of the same group of properties. This is why we do have confidence in arguments from analogy, and why this confidence is much increased as the analogy is shown to be closer and closer. This fact of our experience is discussed in chapter 4, section iv, where we consider the assumptions we make when using arguments from analogy and inductive arguments.

(ii) Interdependence of Induction and Analogy

Inductive arguments and arguments from analogy are interdependent. In an argument from analogy there must be *at least two instances*, that is, at least two objects or events, though the strength of the *analogical* argument will depend on the number of established likenesses. (It will also depend on the relevance of these likenesses to the argument – see previous section – but this point is irrelevant here.) Now an inductive argument is a generalisation based on numbers of instances, but all of these instances must have *at least two properties in common*, though the strength of the argument will depend, in part, on the number of instances. (It will also depend on the variety of those instances; this will be considered in the next section.) Take a simple generalisation 'All crows are black'. This inductive generalisation is based on an inductive argument, the premises of which are descriptions of observations of crows, namely. 'This crow is black', 'That crow is black', etc. But these instances, the crows, must have at least one property, apart from blackness, by which they are recognised *as crows*. In fact they have many properties in common, the possession of distinctively shaped wings, beaks, claws etc, but there *must* be at least one property (apart from blackness) which is the basis for the instance being a crow. Taking an example from science, we have what may be regarded as the inductive generalisation that all samples of chlorine gas are green.* But those samples must have some property other than greenness by which the gas is recognised *as* chlorine gas. The distinctive property may be the bleaching of litmus paper, or the smell, or the reaction producing iodine from an iodide solution, but there must be at least one property common to all the instances, apart from the property which is being inferred by induction.

Thus there can be no *purely* inductive argument and no *purely* analogical argument. One can only say that some arguments are more of one type than another. Analogical arguments are those where emphasis is put on the number of resemblances between what may well be a very limited number of things – it may be of only two things, but it must be at least two. Inductive arguments are those in which the number of instances predominates over the likenesses between the instances, but there must be at least two properties which all these instances have in common.

(*iii*) Positive and Negative Analogy

The likenesses between the instances in an inductive argument are called their *positive analogy*. There must be at least two known likenesses, but in practice there are usually many more: there are many likenesses between different crows and between different samples of chlorine gas. There are many likenesses *of which we are aware*, but it is almost certain that there are yet more likenesses of which we are unaware, and which we therefore, of necessity, disregard. This means that the *total* positive analogy between the instances is almost certain to be bigger than the known, acknowledged, positive analogy.

* The word 'chlorine' is derived from the Greek word for green. Davy so named the gas on account of its colour. But it is unlikely that he thought of the colour as a defining property. If it were then it would be held that the gas could not be chlorine unless it were green. As stated in chapter 1, section ii, and as will be discussed in chapter 5, section i, inductive generalisations, and theories explaining such generalisations, enable us to possess concepts. Generalisations which begin as inductive generalisations may *become* part of a definition; or they may become explained by theories and achieve the status of scientific laws (see chapter 6, sections i and ii). Today we take it to be a scientific law that chlorine gas is green, but originally this was not the case.

Any difference between instances, even if it is only one instance among them which has some different property, is called the *negative analogy*. Thus if only one of the crows ever observed came from a country outside England, if one only was known to have some distinctive cereal in its diet, if one only were kept in a cage whereas others were wild, the negative analogy between the instances would have been increased. It follows that by increasing the variety of our instances we extend the negative analogy and reduce the positive analogy. It is very important to do this, because, if the instances have much in common, that is, if the positive analogy is great because there is very little variety, we may unwittingly be choosing instances that have a likeness in common which, though unacknowledged, is essential to the truth of the inductive generalisation. For example, if all the observed instances of black crows were English crows, it might be essential that crows were English if they were to be black. By observing a French crow and finding that it also is black, we have shown that the Englishness of crows is not essential to the truth of the generalisation. If we observe an American crow and find that it also is black, we have shown that crows need not be of European origin for the generalisation 'All crows are black' to be true.

A famous example of the effect of enlarging the variety of instances is the refutation, or rather modification, of the generalisation 'All swans are white'.* This generalisation was supported by a large number of instances, but these instances showed a positive analogy which had been disregarded as unimportant: the swans were all of European origin. Then black swans were observed in Australia. Now had these swans been white, the new instances would have strengthened the induction because there would have been increased negative analogy – that is, the *difference* between the instances. As it happened the inductive generalisation had to be qualified to 'All swans of the northern hemisphere are white'. So mere number of instances supporting a generalisation is not so important a factor as variety of instances. One properly established instance† which is known to differ from all the others, for example, one black crow from Mongolia,

---

* Of course we could keep our generalisation true by insisting that only white birds could be called swans (see previous footnote). However we then no longer have an inductive generalisation but a definition. (See also chapter 6, sections i and ii.)

† Because it is important that the new observation should be well-established, it is not unlikely that several observations of the new variety of instance will be made. One new instance, particularly if it refutes the generalisation, may be regarded as arising from some mistaken or prejudiced observation. (See also chapter 6, section i.)

is more valuable than dozens of instances which appear to be exactly alike, for example, a hundred black crows from a wood in Surrey.

Any generalisation will explicitly refer to much less than the total positive analogy, that is – the total number of likenesses common to the instances – which, as explained, will not even be known in its entirety. We cannot say how much of the disregarded and/or unknown positive analogy is irrelevant. All that we *know* to be irrelevant are the properties of the negative analogy. By seeking a variety of instances we extend the negative analogy and so show that more and more properties, which *before* the new instance were part of the positive analogy and which *might* have been relevant, are in fact irrelevant. However, because we cannot know the total positive analogy, we cannot completely disregard numbers of instances which appear to be alike. The method of indiscriminate observation of a large number of instances is a sign of weakness, that is, if the instances are not selected to enlarge the negative analogy, but though these instances may not add to our knowledge, there is always the chance that some disregarded positive analogy will be shown to be relevant. This is because no two instances can be *exactly* alike, even though they may appear to be so. Two apparently identical instances will differ in some points, and this *may* prove important.

For example, in 1892 it was shown by an English scientist, Lord Rayleigh (1842–1919), that a sample of nitrogen gas, prepared by removing carbon dioxide, oxygen, water vapour, and the various known impurities from atmospheric air, was not identical with nitrogen which had been prepared by chemical means, such as the heating of ammonium nitrite; it was more dense. In other respects the samples of gases appeared to be alike, and it had been assumed that the densities were the same before Rayleigh's investigation. Rayleigh was eventually able to show that there were traces of other gases in the sample of 'atmospheric nitrogen'. It was in this way that the rare gases: helium,* argon, krypton and others were discovered on the earth.

Examination of apparently identical instances will, in any case, enlarge the negative analogy. Clearly if we know *how* an instance has enlarged the negative analogy we have strengthened the argument decisively. But even if we do not know how we have enlarged it, and indeed can only surmise that it must have been enlarged to some extent, we have certainly done the argument no harm, and, in a very

---

* A curious spectral line had already been noted in sunlight, which was later shown to be helium.

limited way, we have made it more reliable. Thus, when we say that mere numbers of instances are not unimportant, this is because they must increase, to some slight extent, the negative analogy. Occasionally, as in the above example, they reveal an essential positive analogy. Therefore to strengthen the argument it *is* permissible to add to the numbers of instances indiscriminately; but the strengthening effect is not very great. The argument is generally strengthened much more by choosing instances which will extend the negative analogy.

It must be emphasised that enlarging the negative analogy is not the final aim of either experimental science or inductive investigation. We seek to enlarge the negative analogy because we wish to find which part of the positive analogy is essential to the generalisation. In other words, what *must* the instances have in common in order that the generalisation be true? When we take a new instance, which is known to differ from all the other instances in a particular way, and we find that the generalisation still holds, then we can say that the particular property which, before the observation was part of the positive analogy, was an inessential part of that positive analogy,* for example, the fact that all black crows were of English origin was shown to be an inessential part of the analogy between the instances which supported the generalisation 'All crows are black', when it had been shown that French crows were also black. On the other hand, if the inductive generalisation does not apply to the new case, for example, 'All swans are white' does not apply to Australian swans, the generalisation must be qualified. Observation of the new instance reveals an essential feature of the positive analogy, and, though our generalisation has to be qualified, our knowledge of the world has been increased. (See p. 136–7 for Questions and Further Reading related to this chapter.)

---

* Seeking an essential positive analogy by increasing variety of instances is similar to seeking necessary condition by the method of agreement. See analysis of this in chapter 7, section iv.

3

Observation and Experiment

(1) Critical Observation

Scientists observe and also conduct experiments in order to test hypotheses, that is, in the expectation of confirming or refuting hypotheses. Observation is passive in the sense that there is no interference with external events. (We are here disregarding observation of sub-atomic phenomena.) In this respect it may be contrasted with experimentation. Experimentation requires a manipulation of events; it involves arrangement of conditions in order to produce situations which would not otherwise occur. Experimentation of course includes observation, but it involves something more, for, with a hypothesis to guide him, the scientist plans to be able to observe effects which could not be observed in the ordinary or 'natural' course of events.

However, it is not always possible to manipulate events, and so critical observation plays an important role in scientific enquiry. Perhaps the most obvious field in which experimentation is not possible is that of astronomy. The scientist cannot affect the movement of the heavenly bodies; all he can do is to observe them. But he can select those parts of the heavens, and those times, which will best suit his purpose. For example, when the German astronomer Kepler (1571–1630) was attempting to test various hypotheses relating to the paths of the planets, he decided to study the movements, that is the position at various times, of the planet Mars.

Kepler used the very accurate observations which had been made by a slightly older astronomer, Tycho Brahe. Adopting a hypothesis,

Kepler could *calculate* what the position of the planet would be, or had been, at certain times. He could then observe, or check the records, to see whether the planet did occupy, or had occupied, the positions calculated. If there was agreement between calculation and observation, the hypothesis was confirmed; if there was no agreement, the hypothesis was refuted. Kepler's original hypothesis was that the orbit was circular; this had to be abandoned because the observations (those of Tycho Brahe) were not compatible with such an orbit. After attempts at fitting the positions observed to an ovoid path, Kepler finally arrived at the hypothesis that the orbit was that of an ellipse, and this was confirmed by the observations. He then suggested, as a further hypothesis, that other planets also had elliptical orbits. Many subsequent observations have confirmed this hypothesis, and later it was also, in a measure, confirmed by Newton's theory of gravitational attraction: see chapter 5, section iii. *

This is an example of the hypothetico-deductive method. A hypothesis is suggested; there follows a deduction or calculation which indicates what is *expected* to be observed if the hypothesis is correct. It is hoped that observation will be in accordance with what has been calculated or deduced. If observation is in accordance with calculation or deduction, the hypothesis is said to be confirmed; if observation is *not* in accord the hypothesis stands to be refuted and the scientist must think again. The hypothetico-deductive method will be discussed more fully in chapter 4, section vii, but it should be pointed out here that although there is no mention of induction in the account of the method, this does not mean that inductive inference has been avoided. The fact that the hypothesis is confirmed (or refuted) by observation would be of little value if we did not generalise and infer, by induction, that the hypothesis would continue to be confirmed (or refuted) by like observation in the future. Having confirmed that the path of Mars was that of an ellipse, Kepler inferred, again by induction, that it would continue in an elliptical path. The further hypothesis, that other planets would also have an elliptical path, is an argument from analogy. The planets are known to be alike in some respects: for instance, they all move round the sun, and none of them has light of its own. By analogy, it is inferred that, if one planet has an

* In fact, the orbits are not perfect ellipses because each planet is affected by the mass of the other planets as well as by the sun. But Tycho Brahe's observations were not accurate enough for Kepler to detect the discrepancy. The data he had were just accurate enough for him to propose the elliptical orbit: see also this chapter, section v.

elliptical orbit, then so will the others. In so far as all arguments from analogy involve some induction (see chapter 2, section ii), there is also induction in this inference.*

We may study another application of critical observation in scientific enquiry by considering Einstein's confirmation of the General Theory of Relativity. From that theory it is possible to deduce that the paths of the planets round the sun should be that of rotating rather than stationary ellipses. In the nineteenth century, the French astronomer Leverrier had found that the orbit of the planet Mercury showed a rotation round the sun. Einstein calculated that the amount of the rotation corresponded to that which would be expected if his theory were correct. Einstein also predicted that light rays would be curved rather than straight when passing near to massive objects like the sun, which exerted a high gravity field. The sun should therefore bend light coming from the stars. The bending was measured during a solar eclipse, and Einstein's theory was again confirmed. Also, from Einstein's theory it is possible to predict that the spectral lines of elements in a massive body will be shifted towards the red end of the spectrum. Observation shows that spectral lines of certain elements in the sun do show a shift to red, therefore confirming the theory once more. Thus we see that critical observation can help in the establishment of very fundamental theories; *planned* experimentation is not necessarily essential.

Another field in which critical observation rather than experimentation is used is the field of social science, or rather the social sciences. Here again it may be physically impossible to manipulate events. Also, in certain cases, as in seeing the effect of depriving the market of a vital commodity, it may be morally impossible even if not physically impossible, to manipulate events. To study the role of critical observation in such cases we may take the investigations (by Francis Galton (1822–1911) into the efficacy of prayer.† In this case Galton was testing the hypothesis that prayer was of value *in achieving what was prayed for*. It is to be emphasised that he was *not* investigating the value of prayer to the person praying; this would be a matter for psychological rather than sociological investigation.

---

* As indicated above, the elliptical path of the planets may be said to be deduced from Newton's theory of gravitational attraction; so it is not in fact necessary to rely on the argument from analogy. At least, it is not necessary for *us* to rely on it; but it was for Kepler.

† Galton's *Statistical Enquiries into the Efficacy of Prayer* was published in 1872.

Galton said that if the hypothesis that prayer was efficacious was true, then something regularly prayed for would come about. This is a deduction from the hypothesis. The hypothesis will therefore be confirmed if it can be shown that prayer *is* successful in achieving what is prayed for. In the nineteenth century, when people went regularly to church, there would be many people praying each Sunday for the good health and longevity of the Queen and members of the royal family. Galton observed the recorded and well-established facts of the age attained by royalty at death, and compared these with the equally well-established facts as to the age at death of the members of the higher social classes. If royalty could be shown to live longer than the others then it would seem that prayer might be efficacious, but in fact, royalty seemed to fare worse. On average, members of the royal family lived from two to six years less than members of the aristocracy, the gentry, the army and navy, and members of the various professions. It might appear that the hypothesis that prayer was efficacious in bringing about the object prayed for had been quite decisively refuted.

However, a hypothesis or theory is not refuted so easily, and this is why observation must be alert and critical. It could well be argued that prayers for the royal family were not sincere and that many of the prayers offered were made by unworthy people, albeit regular church-goers! Perhaps only sincere prayer from devout people could be efficacious. To allow for this not unreasonable objection, Galton decided to study the efficacy of the prayers of the clergy for their own babies. No one could doubt that prayers for babies would be sincere, and few would go so far as to say that the bulk of the clergy were not devout. Were still-births therefore less frequent among the clergy than among the professional classes generally? (It would not have been good policy to include records of the labouring classes, even if these had been obtainable, for their standard of living was so low.) Galton examined the announcements of births and still births in the *Record*, a clerical newspaper, and in *The Times*; he found that there were the same proportions of still births to live births for clerical families as there were for others.

But perhaps his most telling refutation of the theory was revealed in the observations he made on the practice of insurance companies in obtaining information on which they based their annuity rates. He noted that before insurance companies accepted a life for insurance, they made confidential enquiries as to the health and past medical history of the applicant, but such questions as 'Does he habitually use family prayers and private devotions?' were never asked. Yet, if prayer were expected to prolong life and health, it would be expected that annuity rates for the devout would be higher than for the profane.

All in all, the observations made by Galton (observations critically selected, with objections to certain types of observation being noted), do not confirm the theory that prayer is efficacious in bringing about the object prayed for. They also show that critical observation has a valuable part to play in scientific enquiry. It can help to confirm and to refute theories as surely as can active experimentation.

There is yet another function of observation which is of great importance in science, namely the observation of anomalies or unusual events or phenomena. An anomaly may consist of an unusually high or low proportion of cases with some particular property. It may be noted when facts are being classified in some social investigation. This type of anomaly was observed by Semmelweiss (see next section). We may note that it was observation of another unusual event, the death of a friend in exceptional circumstances, which gave Semmelweiss the clue to an explanatory hypothesis which would account for the original anomaly he had observed. A chance anomaly may also be observed in the course of an actual experiment; this type of anomaly was observed by Priestley (see this chapter, section iii). Anomaly may sometimes be observed during a routine investigation; we have seen (chapter 2, section iii) how Rayleigh noticed the anomaly that nitrogen obtained from the air was more dense than nitrogen prepared by chemical action on nitrogen compounds. In all these cases, and in many others, the observation of the anomaly prompted further hypotheses and further research. But anomalies are not observed by those who are merely lucky. They are only observed by those who have experience of the subject, so that they know what is *expected* and, therefore, what can be taken as anomalous.

Critical observation has then a further function. Not only can it be used to *test* hypotheses; it may also prompt the experienced and alert scientist to make new hypotheses to explain an anomaly. Also the observation of an anomaly may provide a clue to a new explanatory hypothesis.

(ii) Active Experimentation

Critical observation may be supplemented by active experimentation. In experimentation the scientist consciously manipulates events. He has a guiding hypothesis which will determine his arrangement of the situation. The hypothesis may be confirmed or refuted, but in either case his enquiry has been furthered. The value of active experimentation in supplementing critical observation may be appreciated by studying the investigations of the nineteenth-century Viennese gynaecologist, Semmelweiss.

Semmelweiss observed that women who were delivered of babies in the First Maternity Division of his hospital differed from women who were delivered in the Second Maternity Division, and in Vienna generally, in being much more likely to contract a serious and often fatal illness known as puerperal fever. In 1844 the death rate in the First Division was 8.2 per cent, in 1845 6.8 per cent, in 1846 11.4 per cent, whereas in the nearby Second Division, and in Vienna generally, the death rate was between 2 and 3 per cent. Semmelweiss's problem was to find out what it was about the cases in the First Division which produced this unusually high death rate. We might say that he wished to find the essential positive analogy for the patients in the First Division.

It is to be emphasised that Semmelweiss had discovered that there was an anomaly, namely an abnormally high death rate from puerperal fever, in the First Division. He had not dismissed the figures as being due to chance fluctuations. This in itself shows his experience of diseases generally. It is an example of the type of critical observation which was noted at the end of the last section, that is, the critical observation which is alert to the strange or anomalous result, and which prompts the scientist to suggest an explanatory hypothesis.

However, having noted the anomalous figures, Semmelweiss also needed experience to be able to suggest what might possibly be the important and relevant difference between the First Division cases and all the others in Vienna. He decided that he would use his Second Division cases as 'controls' or standard cases because he could control arrangements in the hospital, that is, it was a field in which he could experiment. He compared his First Division cases with those in the Second Division.

He first considered the chance that there was an epidemic infection in the First Division, but decided that this could not be the case because, in the course of months, the epidemic would have died down and/or would have spread to the Second Division. He also discounted a suggestion that the higher death rate was due to overcrowding. The Second Division was *more* crowded than the First Division because patients, knowing the reputation of the First Division, made great efforts to avoid it and to enter the Second Division. Difference in diet could be discounted, for patients received the same food in both Divisions. It was also suggested that patients in the First Division were more roughly treated by the medical students than were the patients in the Second Division, who were attended by midwife nuns. Semmelweiss did not accept this, since both medical students and midwives received the same training. Therefore none of these factors needed to be altered. When considering what conditions to change, Semmelweiss had other hypotheses in mind.

He first entertained the hypothesis that perhaps the manner of delivery affected the death rate. In the Second Division patients were delivered on their sides, whereas in the First Division they were supine. Semmelweiss therefore ordered that patients in the First Division should also be delivered on their sides. This made no difference to the high death rate, so the hypothesis that the method of delivery was responsible was refuted. Then a hypothesis involving psychological causes was suggested. In the First Division a priest taking the sacrament to a dying woman had to pass through five wards before reaching the patient. The dramatic appearance of the priest, who followed an attendant ringing a bell, might perhaps frighten other patients, and this might make them more likely to contract the fever. The patients in the Second Division were not alarmed in this way because the priest could go directly to a dying woman. Semmelweiss persuaded the priest to come to the First Division patients without going through the wards and without the bell-ringing attendant, but the mortality rate did not decrease. So this hypothesis had to be rejected.

Other hypotheses were similarly refuted. Then at last, in 1847, Semmelweiss got a new clue. It was an accident which was responsible for prompting a new hypothesis. One of Semmelweiss's colleagues was punctured by a scalpel whilst doing an autopsy, and he died, displaying the symptoms of puerperal fever. At this time nothing was known about the role of bacteria in infection, but Semmelweiss thought that dead tissue from the corpse (what he called cadaveric matter), might have caused the infection and death. Semmelweiss knew that the medical students came direct from the dissecting room when they attended women in labour. He therefore ordered all his students to wash their hands in chloride of lime before they attended patients in the maternity ward. He knew chloride of lime as a bleaching agent which would destroy cadaveric matter. After this order the mortality rate in the First Division at once decreased, and in 1848 reached 1.27 per cent as compared with 1.33 per cent in the Second Division. Semmelweiss's hypothesis was confirmed.

By patient experiment, guided by experience and insight, Semmelweiss was able to reveal a *significant* difference between the First and Second Division cases. The essential positive analogy among the First Division cases was that they were examined by medical students who had been dissecting corpses. The investigation required methodical and carefully planned experiments, but it also needed judgement and imagination to decide which factors were to be varied, and to take advantage of clues which less experienced and/or less imaginative investigators might have disregarded. The explanation seems glaringly obvious to us today, but it was not obvious at all in the nineteenth century. This, after all, was the first time that contact with corpses had been firmly linked to infection. The conclusion was the result of critical observation and planned experiment.

Semmelweiss, indeed, extended his experiments in a way which would not be tolerated in Vienna today. Having established that cadaveric matter caused a fatal infection, he experimented to establish a general principle of the carrying of infection by diseased tissue. He and his colleagues examined a woman who was dying of a festering cervical cancer, and then, without washing, they examined twelve other women who were not infected. All these twelve women then died of puerperal fever. The hypothesis had been confirmed, but at the expense of twelve lives.

In sociological and medical investigations it is possible to manipulate the events to some extent, but we do not now consider that Semmelweiss's experiment is justified. Today he would have had to be content with infecting animals, and, even so, would have required special permission. Likewise many psychological experiments are carried out on animals because it would not be morally justifiable to conduct analogous experiments on human beings. Also, because animals come to maturity more quickly and so it is possible to obtain results of experiments on development more quickly than human beings it is possible to carry out observation of several consecutive generations, and so test hypotheses which suggest inheritance of characteristics.

However, even in experiments with animals, there are many practical and moral limitations on the manipulation that is possible, and is permitted. It is in the physical sciences physics and chemistry, that there is most scope for active experimentation. The scientist in these fields can manipulate events as he wishes, with a view to producing some desired result or discovering whether a particular event will occur. No experiment is carried out without some expectation; the scientist does not idly alter conditions with no idea as to what may happen, or as to what he hopes (or fears) may happen. He is always guided by some hypothesis, even if it is one which is vaguely formulated. It is true, as we have already seen, that some chance event may be observed which may be the inspiration for some new hypothesis. As we shall see, this is why many scientists have great regard for the occurrence of chance events, and for anomalies. But chance events are helpful only to those who are aware of the regularity. Moreover, even when an anomaly is recognised as an anomaly, further knowledge is needed to suggest an explanation.

Not all hypotheses arise as explanations of anomalies. Very often a scientist will start from a vague common-sense hypothesis with the aspiration of giving a more definite and explicit formulation. For instance, it had been observed that certain calcareous earths, such as limestone, fizz violently when acids are added to them. Joseph Black (1728–99), a Scottish physician and scientist, carried out various experiments to show the relation of the earths to alkalis and the effects produced by the gas evolved in the fizzing.

Black started his investigation with a mild white powder known as *magnesia alba*, or *magnesia**. He chose this substance originally because he appreciated that it had properties in common with limestone and the calcareous earths, and he thought that it might be more effective than lime or lime water in alleviating the pain caused by gall stones. In this he was disappointed, but he was led to other investigations.

Having given full details of his method of preparing magnesia, Black described its reaction with various acids:

> Magnesia is quickly dissolved with violent effervescence, or explosion of air, by the acids of vitriol, nitre, and of common salt, and by distilled vinegar; the neutral saline liquors thence produced having each their peculiar properties.

* Black's terms will be used. What he calls *magnesia alba*, *magnesia*, or *crude magnesia* is our magnesium carbonate. For us magnesia is magnesium oxide, which is formed when magnesium carbonate is strongly heated. Black calls this substance *calcined magnesia*.

We should note that by 'air', Black did not mean the atmospheric air which he would have called 'common air'; the term 'air' signified what is conveyed by our term 'gas'. A *gas* was an *air* to Black and to most of his eighteenth-century contemporaries.

Further experiments revealed that magnesia would loose weight on heating and that heated or calcined magnesia no longer effervesced with acids; Black was careful to weigh his materials:

> An ounce of *magnesia* was exposed in a crucible for about an hour to such heat as is sufficient to melt copper. When taken out it weighed three drams and one scruple, or had lost 7/12 of its former weight.
>
> I have repeated, with the *magnesia* prepared in this manner, most of the experiments I had already made upon it before calcination, and the result was as follows.
>
> It dissolves in all the acids, and with these composes salts exactly similar to those described in the first set of experiments: but what is particularly to be remarked, it is dissolved without any of the least degree of effervescence.

The obvious conclusion was that the loss of weight on heating was due to the loss of the 'air'.

> Observing *magnesia* to lose such a remarkable proportion of its weight in the fire, my next attempts were directed to the investigation of this volatile part. . . .

> Chemists have often observed, in their distillations, that part of a body has vanished from their senses, notwithstanding the utmost care to retain it; and they have always found, upon further inquiry, that subtile part to be air, which having been imprisoned in the body, under a solid form, was set free and rendered fluid and elastic by the fire. We may therefore conclude, that the volatile matter, lost in calcination of *magnesia*, is mostly air; and hence the calcined *magnesia* does not emit air, or make an effervescence, when mixed with acids.

Then Black tried the effect of adding the salt formed from calcined magnesia and acid, to mild alkali (the latter was known to effervesce with acid). An insoluble material was produced which was exactly like the original magnesia, that is, before it had been calcined. Moreover, the newly formed magnesia was almost exactly equal in weight to the weight of the original magnesia. The slight discrepancy could be accounted for (see below). There were further experiments with weighed samples. Black found that whether before or after heating, a given weight of magnesia required practically the same weight of acid to dissolve it. He accounted for the slight weight difference very readily:

> As in the separation of the volatile from the fixed parts of bodies, by means of heat, a small quantity of the latter is generally raised with the former;. . . . This is probably the reason why calcined *magnesia* is saturated with a quantity of acid somewhat less than what is required to dissolve it before calcination: and the same may be assigned as one cause which hinders us from restoring the whole of the original weight, by solution and precipitation.

Black concluded that though crude and calcined magnesia looked different, they differed only in that the crude magnesia contained a considerable quantity of 'air'.

Such a discovery encouraged Black to speculate further. He wondered whether the extra weight that metals gained when they dissolved in acids, and were then precipitated by mild alkalies, might not be due to 'air' furnished by the alkali. (He was correct; a mild alkali, for example, sodium carbonate, would precipitate the carbonate of the metal from a solution of its salt.)* He also concluded, on the basis of further experiments, that the relation between the calcareous earths, such as limestone and lime, was the same as that between crude and calcined magnesia.

Black's experiments are examples of some of the earliest work in chemistry, which indicate appreciation of specifying methods of preparation of materials, and the relevance of knowledge of weights of materials. But we are here concerned to emphasise two points. Firstly, as with all experimentation, there is the necessity for having some hypothesis, some expectation as to the outcome of the experiment. The expectation may not be fulfilled but it has guided the work. Secondly we see that in investigations of this sort, experimentation is essential. In investigating the changes of chemical compounds, mere observation, however critical, is not enough. It is necessary to adjust circumstances (for example, to exaggerate the rise of temperature and the strength of the acid) that occur in natural changes in order to

* This explanation is given in terms of present-day chemistry.

discover more about chemical compounds. Experimentation can take us further than mere observation in our understanding of physical processes.

(iii) Chance Anomaly Prompting Experiment

Reference has already been made to the value of critical observation of chance anomalies. A new instance, which the scientist anticipates will be like a group of previously observed instances but which turns out differently, must increase his knowledge of the world, even if the anomaly cannot be explained. But there will of course be a further increase of knowledge if some explanation can be found. In other words, the scientist will learn more if the anomaly prompts him to devise an explanatory hypothesis which subsequent tests confirm. So important can chance anomaly be that many scientists have thought chance to be more important than any hypothesis. We may cite, for example, the statement of Joseph Priestley (1733–1804), the English natural philosopher who first isolated oxygen:

> It can hardly be too often repeated . . . that more is owing to what we call *chance*, that is . . . to the observation of *events arising from unknown causes*, than to any proper *design*, or preconceived *theory*.

He then affirmed that, at the beginning of his experiments on 'airs', he had no hypothesis that would have led him to his discoveries.

But Priestley was not analysing his, or any scientist's, method of working correctly. It is necessary to distinguish between having no hypothesis at all, and starting with an imprecise hypothesis which may be very unlike the final hypothesis that explains the anomaly. Priestley is right in so far as there may be no precisely formulated hypothesis, and right in that even the vague hypothesis may not be confirmed by experience; but he is wrong in his implication that a hypothesis is unimportant and that chance alone can often lead the scientist to a correct explanation of events. As has already been pointed out, unless the scientist has some theory as to what to expect, he will not be able to recognise an anomaly.

The scientist does not conduct any experiment without some end in view; he must have some hypothesis or theory as to what he expects, albeit vaguely formulated and possibly incorrect. It is of the essence of science to respond and adjust to observation; but the adjustment must be made *from* some other position which has been determined by an earlier hypothesis. As we shall see, Priestley was indeed dominated by hypotheses – though, being a true scientist, he was eventually able to change his ideas in the light of the observations he made. It was thus that he discovered a previously unrecognised substance: that which we call *oxygen*.

Before his discovery of oxygen, Priestley had prepared many gases. He had also studied different samples of common air and had devised a test with nitric oxide (which *he* called 'nitrous air'), whereby he could assess the relative 'wholesomeness' of different samples of common air. Originally this test had been carried out by seeing how long a mouse could survive in a given sample of air, but Priestley appreciated that, since no two mice were exactly alike, the test was unreliable. The nitric oxide test which he devised was carried out in a eudiometer tube. The wholesomeness of the air could be assessed by the reduction in volume of the gas mixture. (The reason for this, not known by Priestley, was that nitric oxide combines with oxygen to give nitrogen dioxide, a soluble gas, which therefore dissolves in the water at the base of the tube.)* By trial and error with different proportions of common air and nitrous air, Priestley discovered that the best proportion of gases to show 'wholesomeness' was one part by volume of nitrous air to two volumes of common air, or half a measure of nitrous air to one measure of common air. If the air were 'wholesome' the addition of half a measure of nitrous air to a measure of common air in the eudiometer tube led to no increase in the volume of gas in the tube; indeed there was a slight decrease. In other words: $\frac{1}{2}$ measure nitrous air + 1 measure common air = slightly less than 1 measure.†

Priestley had prepared many different gases, and he was aware that heating of metallic compounds might yield a gas. He obtained a new gas in 1774, by heating mercuric oxide, or *mercurius calcinatus (per se)* as he called it. He noted that a candle burned brightly in this gas. At first he thought the gas was nitrous oxide (which he called *phlogisticated nitrous air*); previously he had prepared this phlogisticated nitrous air and had shown that it would support combustion. But he was puzzled that the gas should be obtained from a mercury compound. As is often

---

* In modern terms: $2NO + O_2 = 2NO_2$ (soluble).

† $5NO + \underbrace{8N_2 + 2O_2} = \underbrace{8N_2 + NO} + 4NO_2$

Nitric oxide	Common Air	mixture	(dissolves)
5 vols	10 vols	9 vols.	

Starting with 10 measures of 'common air' we are finally left with 9 measures of a mixture of nitrogen and nitric oxide.

the case with anomaly, the first and indeed the sensible reaction is to suspect some sort of mistake. In this case Priestley repeated his experiment, first with a sample of mercurius calcinatus obtained from his friend Waltire, and then with a sample which he could be sure was pure, coming from the chemist Cadet in Paris. Thus he went to some trouble to get pure samples of this compound; but he still obtained the same gas, that is, a gas which, like his phlogisticated nitrous air, supported combustion. However, he came to the conclusion that the new gas could not be phlogisticated nitrous air; his first hypothesis was rejected. This was because he observed that the new gas did not behave as phlogisticated nitrous air behaved in all respects. But he still did not have any idea that the new gas was fit to be breathed and would support life.

> . . . these facts fully convinced me, that there must be a very material difference between the constitution of the air from mercurius calcinatus, and that of phlogisticated nitrous air, notwithstanding their resemblance in some particulars. But though I did not doubt that the air from mercurius calcinatus was fit for respiration, after being agitated in water . . . I still did not suspect that it was respirable in the first instance; so far was I from having any idea of this air being what it really was, much superior, in this respect, to the air of the atmosphere.

In March 1775 Priestley decided to test the new air for wholesomeness with the eudiometer tube. He took what he had discovered to be the best proportions, namely one measure of the new air to half a measure of nitrous air, and he discovered that the reduction in volume was about the same as he would have had if he had mixed common air with nitrous air. This was a coincidence; it just so happens that pure oxygen will give approximately the same amount of soluble nitrogen dioxide as does common air *if* the proportions are those which Priestley took. Here is an example of a chance effect which actually hinders discovery. Priestley then adopted the hypothesis that the new air was common air:

> After this I had no doubt but that the air from mercurius calcinatus was fit for respiration, and that it had all the other properties of common air. But I did not take notice of what I might have observed, if I had not been so fully possessed by the notion of there

being no air better than common air, . . . the diminution something greater than common air would have admitted!

His hypothesis that he had obtained common air prevented him from appreciating the significance of certain facts, among them being the fact that when nitrous air was mixed with the new air there was a slightly bigger reduction in volume than would have been obtained by mixing nitrous air with common air, in the established proportions. However, though he says that he could not recollect exactly *why* he did so, Priestley put a burning candle into the *tested* mixture. He put a candle into the gas which remained in the eudiometer tube *after* the nitrous air had been added. Had this been the residuum of a test with common air, the candle would have been extinguished, and this is what Priestley, on the basis of his hypothesis, would *expect* to occur. To his surprise he noted that the candle continued to burn. Even so, he was reluctant to abandon his hypothesis that the gas was common air, and he said that he always spoke of the air to his friends as being substantially the same as common air. He decided to make a test with a mouse, he *says* for the satisfaction of others rather than for himself. We may doubt that this is strictly true. It is likely that Priestley himself was troubled by the burning of the candle, for it was, in view of his hypothesis, an extraordinary anomaly. He says:

> I procured a mouse and put it into a glass vessel containing two ounce-measures of the air from mercurius calcinatus. Had it been common air, a full-grown mouse, as this was, would have lived in it about a quarter of an hour. In this air, however, my mouse lived a full half hour; and though it was taken out seemingly dead, it appeared to have been only exceedingly chilled; for, upon being held to the fire, it presently revived, and appeared not to have received any harm from the experiment.

He was confirmed that the new air was as good as common air, but he *still* did not think that it was any better

> because, though one mouse would only live a quarter of an hour in a given quantity of air, I knew it was not impossible but that another mouse might have lived in it half an hour.

However, on reflection he became suspicious. He resolved to try his eudiometer test on the air which the mouse had been breathing. Of course if the air were common air, the residuum from the mouse should have given no reduction in the eudiometer test. To his surprise (Priestley apologises for his frequent repetition of the word 'surprize'), he found that the residuum gave a result better than common air.

Finally he carried out the eudiometer test, using increasing amounts of nitrous air. It became clear that the reduction in volume indicated an air four or five times as good as common air.

> Now as common air takes about one half of its bulk of nitrous air, before it begins to receive any addition to its dimensions from more nitrous air, and this air took more than four half-measures before it ceased to be diminished by more nitrous air, and even five half-measures made no addition to its original dimensions, I conclude that it was between four and five times as good as common air.

Priestley had discovered the gas which we call oxygen.

We have seen how chance results could help Priestley, though they could also hinder him. We may also see how *all the time* his experimentation was guided by his current hypothesis; either he followed the routine the hypothesis suggested, or he investigated an anomaly, that is, a surprising event which his hypothesis did not lead him to expect, or which it even led him not to expect. Sometimes, we may suspect, he was more alert to anomaly than his account suggests. He said that he added the burning candle to the residuum from the mouse by chance, but it is unlikely that such an experiment would have been performed by a man less experienced or less gifted. We have seen that Priestley said he could not recollect what he had in mind when making the experiment, but he may have been half-conscious that the reaction in the eudiometer tube was not quite that which would have been found with common air. What Priestley's account does undoubtedly show is that chance events can only be appreciated as significant if there is considerable background of knowledge, and a current hypothesis indicating what is to be expected.

(iv) Testimony

No one man can carry out all the observations necessary for adequate confirmation of even a single hypothesis. He must rely in good measure on the testimony of others. For example, when Kepler made his calculations to determine the orbit of Mars he used not only his own observations but also those of the Danish astronomer Tycho Brahe (1546–1601), with whom he had worked for some time. The testimony of Brahe was to be preferred to Kepler's own observations, for Kepler believed that Tycho Brahe was the more skilled and accurate observer. Moreover, even if he had been satisfied with the quality and quantity of his own observations, Kepler would have relied on the testimony of others with regard to the reliability of the instruments, the clocks and the sextants, which he used. Even if he had made and designed his own instruments, Kepler would still have had to rely on the testimony of others as to the reliability of the metals and other materials of which those instruments were made.

Consideration of any of the experiments described in the previous chapters will lead us to the conclusion that the testimony of others plays an essential part in any scientific investigation. Einstein, like Kepler, had to rely on the testimony of others: he had to rely on the testimony of others to predict the time of the eclipse, and on testimony as to the observations made during the eclipse. Again, when considering the rotation of the planetary orbits, Einstein relied on Leverrier's calculations as to the rotation of the orbit of Mercury. Leverrier himself probably relied on the testimony of other astronomers when collecting data for his calculations.

It is clear that Galton had to rely on the testimony of others, testimony from many different sources, when compiling his evidence for assessing the efficacy of prayer. He could not personally collect the figures which he took from *The Times* and the *Record*. He could not personally discover the length of life of the individual members of the professional classes, or even of the royal family, and so calculate his own averages.

It might be possible, though not often practicable, to use only our own observations when conducting a single experiment, but when using statistical information we must rely on testimony. Such testimony can and must be critically examined. We must be told the number of cases observed, and what fraction they are of the total; we must try to ascertain that they are a fair sample. When using statistical evidence, we may require the testimony of an expert statistician to assure us that the statistics themselves are reliable. In other words we require testimony to the effect that the initial testimony is valuable. This can be true of all testimony, but it is particularly true of testimony when in statistical form because it may be too difficult for the layman to assess its reliability. Statistics can be technically correct and yet be highly misleading.

But of course there are degrees of reliability in testimonies relating to the occurrence of particular events. We may set aside considerations of testimony which is suspected of being emotionally biased, or prompted by malice or favouritism, as being not within the sphere of science. But we must still allow for the chance of *mistake* in testimony, and for the bias inherent in holding a given hypothesis. Priestley had the testimony of his local pharmacist as to the purity of his original sample of mercurius calcinatus, but he did not value this testimony so highly as that of his colleague, Waltire. He rated the testimony of Cadet, in regard to the purity of chemical compounds, even higher. Though we may be somewhat biased (in favour or against) in assessing the value of the testimony of those we know personally, it is possible to make a reasonably objective assessment of the value of the testimony of a given individual in relation to a given topic. This assessment is related to the proven and established skill and knowledge of the individual. But we cannot be so sure that another's testimony is free of bias, in favour of or against, a hypothesis. Indeed it is arguable that emotions *are* a factor in science, in that a hypothesis can be accepted or rejected with a vehemence which is tantamount to emotional bias. The best that can be hoped is that we should be aware of the danger, to ourselves and others, and so try to avoid it. As stated above, the ideal of science is to disgard emotional attachment to any hypothesis, but since the scientist must always be guided by a hypothesis, it may be impossible for him to be entirely free of emotional involvement.

We take evidence which is attested by many individuals, or even a relatively small number of trained and experienced individuals, as being reliable. Thus, instruments which have been found to be satisfactory by many independent workers, are relied on without question. Even a new instrument, which has been made and designed by a man or firm of good repute, will be used without demur. Again, if the result of an experiment is agreed by many independent scientists, their testimony will be accepted as sound. In such cases it is only if there is some positive reason for being suspicious of some general and perhaps fundamental mistake, that doubt would arise. If this did happen, then it would be necessary to observe more carefully ourselves, or to carry out further experiments to test the previously accepted testimony. Certainly observations which were themselves suspect would not be used as evidence in the course of other investigations.

However eminent and reputable the work of one scientist or one research group may be, their testimony as to the outcome of some new experiment is followed by further investigation. Accounts of scientific experiments are always published with a wealth of practical detail, so that others may repeat the experiment as nearly as possible in the same manner. It is not that the honesty or sincerity of the investigators is doubted, but they may have inadvertently overlooked some feature or features which could effectively nullify the conclusions which have been reached.

For example, Robert Boyle (1627–91) thought that he had conclusively proved that heat had weight. He had heated some tin in a sealed vessel which was weighed before and after heating, and he had discovered that the vessel weighed more after heating. He had concluded that the increase in weight must have come from the heat which had been applied. His testimony, based on what seemed conclusive evidence, was to the effect that heat had weight. At first this testimony had great value, for Boyle was one of the most eminent scientists of his day (and a founder member of the Royal Society). But he had overlooked an important fact. He had had partially to evacuate the vessel to which the heat was applied in order that the expansion of the enclosed air, which would occur on heating, did not crack the walls. After heating, but before reweighing, Boyle had opened the vessel; therefore some air would have entered. The increase in weight which Boyle observed could have been and in fact was due to the entrance of this air, not to the heat.

As another example we may take the testimony of an English Catholic priest, John Needham, in the eighteenth century. He thought that he had shown that micro-organisms were spontaneously generated in living matter. He affirmed that he had obtained micro-organisms from meat broth which had been sterilised and then sealed off from air. His testimony, based on apparently good evidence, was to the effect that life could develop spontaneously in non-living matter. Later it was shown that Needham's sterilisation was inadequate, and so his testimony was false.

We may think that today such mistakes would not be made, but this is being over-confident. It has already been emphasised that it would not be possible to carry out experiments without the guidance of a hypothesis, but hypotheses are potentially dangerous in that they may determine too easily what we take care to observe. We have seen in Priestley's account of his discovery of oxygen, how his conviction that the new gas was but a form of common air hindered him from appreciating the significance of his first eudiometer test, namely that his new air was giving him a result slightly better than that to be expected from common air. The testimony that Priestley gave to his friends at that time was false. It is very likely that present-day hypotheses may be similarly misleading scientists. Mistakes may well be being made which will seem obvious errors to later generations of scientists. This is why even well-established testimony cannot be regarded as beyond question.

Nevertheless it has to be accepted that the vast majority of *facts* which the scientist takes as giving a secure basis to his work are established *as facts* by virtue of testimony, and not by the scientist himself. His own account of his own observations will be testimony which can be used by his colleagues. Observation and experiment are essential to science, but one individual or even one group of individuals cannot rely on these alone. For any scientist, his own single observations may not be so valuable as the testimony of his colleagues. Testimony is an essential constituent of any scientific investigation, and progress would be impossible without it.

(v) Measurement

When any property is measured its value is compared with some standard. We regard properties as being measurable if we are able to suggest a procedure whereby there would be independent agreement among any number of qualified observers as to the value of the property in relation to the standard. Measurements may be performed very accurately with complicated instruments, or very crudely with primitive instruments, but, in relation to the degree of accuracy expected, there must be intersubjective agreement on the measured value if the procedure is to be rated as one of quantitative measurement. In this section we are not concerned with details of accurate measurement, or indeed with practical distinction between accurate and less accurate measurement; we are concerned to discuss the importance of measurement of different properties in the advancement of empirical science.

In the days of the Ancient Greeks only weight, length and time were held to be measureable properties. Today scientists prefer to take 'mass' as a fundamental unit rather than 'weight'. Weight is a property which we can all appreciate directly, but it was shown by Newton that weight is in fact a force. Weight on earth is a consequence of the gravity field of the earth acting on bodies. (There is a reciprocal force which every body exerts on the earth, but because the mass of the earth is so great, these reciprocal forces are negligible.) The concept of mass is sophisticated and we must come to understand it by considering weight. In outer space bodies are weightless, the astronauts have to deal with the problem of weightlessness, but such bodies still have mass. On the moon those same bodies again possess weight, but it is less than the weight on earth because the gravitational field of the moon is weaker than that of the earth. Weight can be regarded as the effect of gravitational fields on bodies which have mass, but mass is fundamental, a property of all material bodies.

For scientists, certain dimensions are chosen as fundamental. By international agreement, there are seven fundamental dimensions. But both the actual dimensions chosen and the number of them is a matter of arbitrary decision. See M. L. McGlashan's text in RIC monograph for teachers entitled *Physics, Chemical Quantities and Units* (2nd edn. 1971). Most of the common physical properties can be expressed in terms of length, mass and time. Taking length as L, mass as M, and time as T, we have:

$$\text{Density} = M/L^3$$
$$\text{Velocity} = L/T$$
$$\text{Acceleration} = L/T^2$$
$$\text{Force} = \text{Weight} = ML/T^2$$
$$\text{Energy} = \text{Heat} = ML^2/T^2 \text{ etc.}$$

Length, mass and time are essentially different concepts, and we shall consider each of them in turn, but we shall find that, though they are each distinctive, and though they arise from different kinds of sense experience, they are measured by the same basic process, namely the coincidence of a mark on some scale with an edge or pointer. *All* measurement, when analysed, depends on this procedure.

Let us first consider the notion of length, for this is most directly related to the fundamental measuring operation. First we must decide on some arbitrary length, say the metre, which is to be taken as the standard unit of length. Earlier standards were based on parts of the body: the foot, the thumb, the length of an outstretched arm. But, though they may seem less arbitrary than the metre, which is defined as 1,656,763.83 wave-lengths of a certain radiation from krypton 86, the decision to adopt *any* size as a unit is and must be arbitrary.* Such a decision must, of course, be taken, and then, having adopted one length as standard, other units of length, which are *defined* as fractions or multiples of the standard, may also be chosen. The millimetre, centimetre, kilometre and so on are all defined by their relation to the metre. It is convenient to have units of several different sizes, for it is better to measure any given property in terms of a unit of appropriate size. It would be highly inconvenient to measure the distance from Exeter to London in millimetres, or even metres, for the number would be so big; it would be highly inconvenient to express the diameter of blood cells in metres because the fraction would be so small. We therefore relate convenient-sized units to our standard. If we eventually have to measure properties which are of a different order of size from those we have measured before, we define a new unit (still in terms of our standard). For example, the *light year* (the distance light will travel in a year) has been adopted for measuring the distances of the stars and nebulae; the pico- or nano-metre has been adopted for measuring the wavelength of radiations emitted by atoms.

Any measured length is not an absolute quantity, it is a ratio. It is a comparison of the length measured with the appropriate standard. When we say that a racecourse is 100 m. long, we are effectively saying that it is 100 times the length of our standard. This is true of all measurements; the measured quantity expresses the relation of that which is measured to the particular standard unit. This is why, in any measurement, the unit with which we are concerned *must* be stated. It is not enough to say that something is length 3; we must say whether it is 3 cm, 3 m, or 3 km.

* It can be argued that some units are more 'arbitrary' than others. The French regarded the metre as in some sense 'natural' and non-arbitrary since it was supposed to be one millionth of the earth's circumference. In fact their calculation of that circumference was incorrect, but even if it had been correct, the decision to adopt that particular fraction of that particular length was arbitrary.

However, as an example of what might be held to be a more arbitrary unit, we have the standard yard of 1834. After the burning of the eighteenth-century standard yard (which had been defined as the length of the second-pendulum, at Greenwich) it was thought convenient *not* to make a new standard by reference to the pendulum but to collect the sub-standards (held at major cities) and to take the average of these for the new standard.

Perhaps the case of some units being more arbitrary than others is analogous to pigs being more equal than other animals.

Length can be measured by placing the standard rod against the object and seeing with what position on the marked scale of the standard the object coincides. The child, measuring the length of a line with his school ruler, illustrates the way in which we *all* measure length. Whether we are measuring tiny distances with the help of a microscope, or astronomical distances with the help of a telescope, the actual measurement must be a matter of finding a coincidence of the measured object against the scale of the measuring instrument.

Much has been made of the desirability of the standard rod being rigid – so that it remains the 'same length', but the rigidity of our standard rod is not so much a matter of necessity as of convenience. There is no *logical* reason for us to avoid using a flexible rod of wax or rubber; we can *define* that rod as the standard. However, if we do decide to take such a rod as the standard, then many *other* objects will be found to have ever-changing lengths. Therefore it will clearly be more convenient and simple to take a standard rod that will be rigid relative to as many other objects as possible, so that as many lengths as possible remain fixed under the same conditions. It has been found that the most 'rigid rod' is one consisting of a certain number of electromagnetic waves (see definition of the metre above), but, though this is our ultimate standard, we also choose sub-standards which are as rigid as possible in relation to the ultimate standard. Again, this is not a logical necessity, but is a matter of convenience. It is much more convenient to take sub-standards which can be simply related to the ultimate standard.

We know that, in relation to our ultimate standard (the wavelength of a certain light), all solids get longer if their temperature rises. Now if we had chosen a metal rod as our *ultimate* standard we would not be under a *logical* necessity to specify the temperature but it would be very inconvenient not to insist that it should be the standard length *at a certain temperature*. For, if we did not so insist, we should find that, as the temperature rose, the lengths of many objects, as measured by our standard, would change, and different objects, made of different materials, would change by different amounts. The size of any given object would therefore depend on the temperature of the standard rod and the actual fluctuations would vary for different materials. There is no logical reason to prevent our having a standard rod which would result in this effect, but it is clear that it would make measurement itself, and physical laws involving the measurement, extremely complicated.

The notion of measuring mass is not as easy as the notion of measuring length, since the concept of mass is much more sophisticated than the concept of length. Length can be directly sensed, but we have seen that mass is inferred from weight. On this earth all things which have mass have weight as a result of the gravitational field. For our purpose here we can take it that mass is directly proportional to weight, and *on this earth* we can regard measurement of mass as being directly obtainable from measurement of weight. Weight can be sensed and can be measured by direct relation to standard units. A standard unit of weight can therefore be regarded as a standard unit of mass.

We pick one standard unit of mass, and then decide to define smaller and larger units in order to measure different sizes conveniently. The basic weighing process, the process analogous to the placing of a ruler along a line, is the balancing of two pans, one containing the standard weights and the other containing the object to be weighed. We know that there is equality when an indicator marks an agreed point on the scale between the pans. There are, of course, very delicate instruments for weighing tiny masses, and other instruments for weighing the enormous masses of the heavenly bodies, but they must all finally be matched against a standard by the coincidence of a pointer on a scale mark. The acutal process, whereby we judge that a given mass is a certain ratio of the standard mass, is the same as the process by which we judge that a given length is a certain ratio of the standard length. Again we should note that any measured mass is a ratio and that it is essential that the unit used should be stated.

Time is a property entirely different from either length or mass, and the concept of time is entirely independent of the concepts of length or of mass. Indeed it is not usual to think of *time* as a property of objects; it is held to be more a property of events. Though time is quite independent of length and mass, there is again a similar procedure in the process of measurement. As with the two other properties a standard must be decided upon. Today the basic unit of time is the period of vibration of the caesium atom; other periodic times, such as the swing of a pendulum, or the rotation of the earth in relation to the dog star, Sirius, can be related to and expressed in terms of the fundamental unit. As with the choice of fundamental measuring rod, there is no *logical* necessity to choose what might be described as a relatively 'rigid periodicity', but it is more *convenient* to choose a standard which is constant or 'rigid' in relation to many other periodic processes. When this is done, the various periodic processes can be simply related to the standard, just as different objects made of different materials can have their lengths simply related to the rigid measuring rod. Again, as far as the *procedure* of measurement of time goes, we shall find that the operation involves watching for the coincidence of a pointer with a scale mark. The pointer may be a clock hand rather than a ruler, but the practice of seeking coincidence is behind the measurement.

Now why is it that all these properties – length, mass and time – are measurable? Why is it that independent inter-subjective agreement can be obtained as to their value in any given circumstance? It is that two like properties, that is two lengths, can be physically put together to give a new value of the property which is the *sum* of the original two. Different values of the property can be added or subtracted according to the ordinary rules of arithmetic. For example, if one length is put in a straight line with another length, the resulting straight line will have a length which is the arithmetical sum of the two original lengths. If one mass is taken from another mass, the resulting mass has a value which is the arithmetical difference of the value of the original two masses. For time the situation is different in that it is not possible literally to *put* one period next in time to another period; but if the one period of time is measured subsequent to another period, the total of time measured will be equal to the sum of the two periods.

These facts about length, mass and time are empirical facts in so far as they are not logically necessary; they are not an *essential* feature of the original concepts. It is possible to imagine a world where length is no more additive than beauty, and, indeed, unless we specify that our lengths must be in one straight line, it is not correct to say that lengths may be arithmetically added. However, *having decided to measure length, mass and time in a given way*, we must admit that the additive feature of the properties *has become* logically necessary. It is because we conceive of the concepts in a certain way that they are measureable. It is because the Ancient Greeks did not conceive of *other* properties in an analogous way that they thought that other properties were not measurable. The Greeks thought that it would not be possible to obtain inter-subjective agreement as to the values of these other properties. It was the basis of a great advance in empirical science, that is, in our knowledge of the empirical world, when new conceptions of properties were proposed, so that these properties did become measurable.

Let us consider a quality such as temperature, which was certainly not considered an additive property by the Greeks. If we take a body at one temperature and add it to a body at another temperature, the resulting temperature is not to be found by adding the two temperatures together. If we mix or juxtapose two bodies at the same temperature, the resulting temperature is not twice the original. However, if we say that the temperature of a given body *rises* by a certain amount, and then that there is a *further rise* in temperature, then it is quite possible to conclude that the total rise in temperature is the sum of the two separate rises. (It is to be noted that by referring to rise in temperature [as opposed to gain of heat] we do not have to allow for change of state. A rise in *temperature* is always additive; it is only if it is being used to calculate a gain in heat that there may be some confusion.) This additive conception of temperature is possible because change in temperature is no longer conceived as a qualitative 'warmer than' or 'cooler than', but as the gain or loss of some property. This view of temperature came about when it was appreciated that change in temperature could be related to change in volume. Rise in temperature could be interpreted as an increase in volume, fall in temperature could be interpreted as a decrease in volume.

It is an empirical fact that whether we measure the change in temperature by change in the volume of a gas, or of a liquid such as mercury or alcohol, we will produce much the same standard scale of temperature. The different scales, based on the expansion of different fluids, are as nearly alike as the scales of length based on iron, copper or silver measuring rods (at constant temperature) would be. There are slight differences, and in fact the 'substance' actually chosen to supply the standard expansion is an ideal or perfect gas, but the choice, just as in the case of other standards, is not prompted by logical necessity, it is prompted by requirements of convenience. A temperature scale based on the expansion of an ideal gas enables physical laws concerning temperature to be expressed most simply.

The concept of temperature as an additive property becomes clearer when a method of measuring is devised and adopted. We may see this more certainly in regard to temperature than with length, mass or time, because we start to measure these properties so early in our lives that the concepts seem intuitively obvious. In fact our concepts of length, mass and time are also intimately related to the operations of measuring these properties. But temperature, which is a property we learn to measure later in life, and more laboriously, is plainly seen to be a concept which is clarified by the process of measurement. When considering temperature, we may note that though the concept of temperature change involves the concept of volume change the actual measurement of that change depends, as always, on the coincidence of the boundary of the measured volume against a scale mark.

The concept of heat was clarified after the concept of temperature. Before an additive view of heat was taken (so that it could be measured), heat was often confused with temperature. The notion of temperature as the *intensity* of heat, so that temperature change could *indicate* heat change, though it was not the same as heat change, was slow to develop. Once we consider that heat is a quantitative property it is not difficult to regard it as an additive property. Heat can be added and subtracted just as length can be; the difference is that it cannot be measured directly. To measure heat we must measure both mass (weight) and temperature, but we also have to know the *specific heat* of the material. This is a sophisticated concept which developed along with the notion of measuring heat by observing temperature changes. It was from attempts to measure heat change in terms of temperature rise, and from observation that different materials showed different rises in temperature when exposed to the same source of heat for the same time, that the concept of specific heat arose.

Consideration of any quality will show that it can be described as a measurable quality when it can be treated as an additive property. Reflection will also indicate that any sort of quantitative measurement must finally depend on the observer seeing the coincidence of the edge or a pointer with a mark on a standard scale. (In this account quantitative measurement is considered – not mere matching, as in matching paint colours, perfume blends, or wine.) These are two basic features common to all measurement, whether we are measuring a line with a child's ruler, or the change in energy levels of an atom.

There are many properties like heat which have values that must be calculated from measurement of other properties – such properties as molecular weight, relative humidity and entropy. But we must not over-emphasise the distinction between such derived properties, and primitive properties which can be measured directly. Only the units of mass, length and time are *fundamental*, and yet mass has to be derived from weight. Again not all properties which can be measured directly would be commonly held to be primitive. Such properties as density, velocity and electrical resistance may all be measured directly if certain instruments are used. The density (at least of liquids) can be measured with a hydrometer; velocity can be measured with a speedometer; electrical resistance can be measured with a Wheatstone bridge. Yet none of these properties are fundamental; they are all derived from other properties.

Nevertheless we can roughly classify properties into two groups: those that are measured by *direct* comparison to some arbitrary value of the property, for example, such properties as weight, length and specific gravity; and those properties which are given a definite value by relating them to some *different*, albeit standard, physical properties, for example, a property such as temperature. The temperature scale is defined by reference to the boiling point of pure water at standard pressure and the melting point of pure ice. Nevertheless, whichever way the standard is found, by direct comparison or by indirect comparison, there will be agreement as to the *value* of any particular property on the scale accepted. This is our touchstone for the possibility of measurement (see the beginning of the chapter).

Now there are some properties which cannot be measured on scales established by either of these two methods. They may be properties which emerge as the result of statistical investigations, for example, the marginal utility of a given commercial product, or they may be properties of an individual, such as beauty or intelligence. In these cases no acceptable standard has been found, and/or there is no method of objectively comparing a given example of the property with a standard.

The Intelligence Quotient, IQ, is the result of an attempt to make an objective scale for measurement of intelligence. It purports to be based on investigations with children where 'mental age' could be related to 'physical age', but the term has had its application extended and can be used to describe adults. However, because the concept of intelligence is so complex, and yet so indistinct, it has not been possible to devise a truly objective scale to which all can agree.

The best we can do is to get a measure of agreement among a group of psychologists on suitable test questions, and then to conduct the test on a considerable number of individuals,* taking the score which

---

* The selection of these individuals is clearly of major importance. Early IQ ratings in England were developed from tests on children at 'Board Schools'. IQ 100 is the average intelligence as assessed from tests on these children. It is thought that the average for a child in a state school today is a little higher than this; so a new set of standardising

is nearest to that of the largest number of individuals in the group as indicating an average IQ of, say, 100. On any given occasion, and in regard to that particular test, we shall be able to produce a scale of *ordering* of IQs which will be reasonably objective, and which will show which individuals are above and which are below average. The ordering will be objective in that, *as far as the particular test is concerned*, all qualified observers will agree on the order. It is analogous to the ordering of temperature which might have been obtained with a primitive expansion thermometer before temperature scales were defined. On any given occasion, the temperature of a set of objects could be objectively ordered by using just that one thermometer. Ordering is a stage on the way to objective measurement; it is objective in a certain definite context but, unlike measurement, it does not give us a value in terms of some absolute standard which is independent of a particular test or particular instrument.

Measurement – true measurement – is important to science because by measurement it is possible to obtain objective assessment of properties. Once objective assessment of properties is obtained, it is possible to compare and relate the values of *different* properties of the same object or material, for instance, the pressure and volume of a gas. It may then be discovered that two different properties are interdependent, in that their values (as objectively assessed in numerical ratios of the standard units) can be related by some arithmetical rule. Measurement of the pressure and volume of gases (at constant temperature) led Boyle to the rule that pressure values and volume values were related by inverse proportion, and therefore led him to the *law* of the interdependence of pressure and volume (temperature being constant). Such a law could lead to better understanding of the behaviour of gases themselves.

Measurement can of course never be more than an approximation. We see the coincidence of a pointer with a mark on a scale, yet we cannot be sure that this coincidence is exact. But today our instruments are so finely balanced and our methods of observation so sophisticated that it is possible for our measurements to give a more accurate description of nature than our generalisations. It has been argued that, in its early stages, accurate instruments may be a hin-

tests would result in a new '100 IQ' norm. Clearly if all the individuals of the standardising sample were from homes for the mentally handicapped, or if all of them were university graduates, we should have different '100 IQ' norms. But whichever norm we decide to take, we can still establish a scale of ordering, if there is agreement as to the reliability of the test questions.

drance to science since it would not then be possible to formulate generalisations which are only approximately true. But, once a generalisation is arrived at, supported by observation with relatively crude instruments, an accurate instrument can reveal that the properties are *not* related as the crude generalisation indicates. It is then more likely that the generalisation needs modification rather than that the measurements or instruments need correcting. However, if instruments had been so accurate at first, the crude generalisation might not have been formulated and even though it is but an approximation, it may yet help knowledge by encouraging the formation of an explanatory theory.*

Numerical laws, such as Galileo's law and Boyle's law, may lead to theories. Such theories may *also* involve numerical relations between theoretical entities. Newton's theory of gravitational attraction postulates forces which are inversely proportional to the square of the distance between them; in the kinetic theory of gases, molecules are postulated with a velocity which has a value dependent on the temperature of the gas. It is from measurement that we obtain numerical laws, and it is from measurement that there arises a mathematical theory which postulates relations in the theoretical zone analogous to relations suggested by laws.

It is to be emphasised that any theory is *more than* a set of mathematical relations between entities postulated by the theory. The mathematical formulae give us a precise and simplified account of how the entities behave in certain explicit conditions, but the theoretical entities themselves are not mere symbols in the equations. The position of theoretical entities, as described by equations, can be compared to the position of phenomena, that is, actual lengths and weights, as described by numerical laws. The law gives a description of how the phenomena behave in certain circumstances, but it does not give a *complete* description of the phenomena. For example, Kepler's law states that the orbit of a planet round the sun is that of an ellipse, but this law does not tell us all there is to know of planets or of the sun. Similarly the kinetic theory of gases suggests certain numerical laws relating kinetic energy of molecules to the temperature of the gas, but this does not mean that the numerical relations tell us all there is to know about molecules.

* See chapter 3, section i; chapter 5, section iv. The orbits of the planets are not *perfect* ellipses but because observation was relatively crude Kepler considered that his hypothesis was confirmed.

Measurement makes it possible for us to mathematise and thus to abstract from experience, so that we simplify experience by codifying it in mathematical form. The mathematics may seem very complicated but, because it is an abstraction, it is very much less complex than the actual world of sense. Simplification by mathematising experience seems to be essential for the progress of science; we cannot understand unless we simplify. But it is well to remember that mathematics is but a means to an end; at the last, the mathematics of science must be related back to sense experience.

As science progresses the relatively simple laws, based on relatively crude measurement, may come to be corrected by theory as well as by more accurate measurement. For example, accurate measurement of gas pressure and volume shows that Boyle's law does not accurately describe the facts. Gas pressure and volume, when accurately measured, are *not* inversely proportional at constant temperature. The kinetic theory of gases is able to account for the discrepancies and to suggest another law, described by Van der Waal's equation, which conforms more closely to the relation between pressure and volume as measured. (This is also discussed in chapter 5, section iv.) Thus measurement can help to establish relatively simple empirical generalisations but it can *also* help us to correct those generalisations and in so doing to confirm explanatory theories.

Measurement may also help the scientist to understand a process. This is particularly so in chemistry. For example, if the law of conservation of mass in chemical reactions is accepted, then the measurement of changes in weight in such reactions may indicate what actual changes in the reactants are taking place. The account of Black's investigations on *magnesia alba*, given in this chapter, section ii, illustrates this.

We may therefore say that measurement has five very important functions in science. First, it allows the scientist clearer concepts of the properties measured than he had before he had devised a method of measurement. Second, it allows properties to be objectively assessed and so prepares the way for empirical generalisations stating objective relations between properties. Third, it leads from this to theories which also assert numerical relations between theoretical entities, and thus leads us to the abstraction and simplification of experience which we require if we are to understand. Fourth, more accurate measurement may support theories that correct laws which are themselves supported by relatively crude measurements. Fifth, measurement can help the scientist to understand the mechanism of particular processes, especially in the field of chemical change.

Hence measurement is no dull routine process; it is not merely a matter of making facts more precise. It is an experimental procedure which is successful because it is planned to accord with the way objects in the world of sense, the empirical world, do actually behave. It can lead the scientist to numerical laws and to that simplification which comes from the mathematisation of experience. But, at the same time, it can enlarge and deepen the scientist's understanding by extending his concepts and also by clarifying them. Also it can prompt and encourage speculation which leads to new explanatory theories. (See pp. 137–8 for Questions and Further Reading related to this chapter.)

4

The Justification of Inductive Inference

(i) Empirical Generalisations and Mathematical Propositions

Having made certain observations on objects in a group or on some set of events, are we justified in making a generalisation about all similar objects or about all similar events? We have good cause to entertain doubts about the truth of any generalisation we may make on the basis of past experience, because it is very likely that the generalisation will need to be qualified, modified or occasionally even fundamentally altered. From experience of common-sense inductions, let alone from consideration of scientific generalisations, we can say any generalisation at present accepted is at best no more than an approximation. From generalisations such as 'All swans are white' to Newton's inverse square law, 'The force between two bodies is proportional to the product of the masses of the two bodies and inversely proportional to the square of the distance between them', there has been a need to make modifications.

However, it is very rare that well-established generalisations, especially those established in science, have to be discarded *completely*. We take it for granted that some appropriate qualification will lead us to a more sound generalisation (though it is unlikely to be immune from *further* qualification). It is one of the aims of science to discover essential positive analogy by discovering a new instance which is an exception to an established generalisation; the exception must lack some feature which is part of the essential positive analogy.

But are we justified in thinking along these lines? Have we any logical reason to expect that there will be a regularity in events and a similarity in the properties of objects? Are we justified in thinking that, if an irregularity is observed in the pattern of events previously established, then there *must* be some additional difference in these events which will account for the observed irregularity? Having established an inductive generalisation on the basis of observation, can we rely on it, or, if it appears to be false, can we rely on there being some factor which will explain the failure of the generalisation?

Generalisations about objects and events in the empirical world must be distinguished from propositions which may have some superficial resemblance to empirical generalisations but which are derived from logical and/or mathematical axioms. For instance, a proposition such as '2 + 2 = 4' or '2 + 2 = 5' must be distinguished from generalisations such as 'All crows are black' or 'All swans are white'. A proposition such as 'In a right-angled triangle the square on the hypotenuse is equal to the sum of the squares on the other two sides' must be distinguished from an empirical law such as 'A body falling freely towards the earth accelerates by 32 feet per second per second' (981 centimetres per second per second)*.

It is sense experience which provides evidence on which to decide on the truth or falsity of empirical generalisations. But in the case of arithmetical propositions and geometrical propositions we need only follow the process of reasoning from the definitions of the terms, and the relations between them, whereby the proposition is arrived at, to come to a conclusion about their truth. Empirical evidence based on sense experience is not required. Observations involving the counting of beans or the drawing of geometrical figures may help us to *understand* mathematical and geometrical propositions but they are not needed to establish the truth of these propositions.

This distinction arises from the fact that these propositions form part of an artificial system which *we* have constructed. The terms in the propositions do not refer to events in the empirical world, they relate only to the axioms and definitions of the constructed system. These axioms and definitions are taken as what might be called arbitrary truths; they are not to be disputed as far as the system is con-

* In the case of freely falling bodies we have reasons, apart from direct observations and measurement, of free fall, to surmise that the acceleration is 32 feet per second per second (981 cm per second per second). But the main point remains, that it is sense experience, not pure reasoning, which supports the law. In the case of empirical laws such as this one, that is, laws which are supported by scientific theories, there are observations other than direct observations, which are involved. (See chapter 5.)

cerned. But, it may be objected, surely mathematics, and especially geometry, tell us and have told us a great deal about the empirical world. We use mathematics to measure areas of land, to calculate the stresses and strains in bridges and buildings, and to help in the derivation and stating of scientific laws and theories. Moreover, the very notion of counting and measuring space arose from experience in the practical matters of the everyday world.

It is true that for centuries it was held that mathematics could give us certain knowledge of the world. Indeed, apart from knowledge granted directly by God, it was believed that mathematical, including geometrical, knowledge was the only certain empirical knowledge. It was admitted that there might never be absolutely accurate measurement, but this was held to be a practical limitation, not a theoretical limitation, of the application of mathematics and, in particular, geometry, to the empirical world. Einstein, however, showed that the space of the world of sense, that is, of the empirical world, was *not* precisely the same as the space of Euclidean geometry. The angles of a 'real' triangle, that is, a triangle drawn on a sheet of paper, do *not* add up to exactly 180°, and this is not due to any fault in drawing, although, for triangles of any size that we can in fact draw, practical errors will mask the discrepancy. Similarly Pythagoras's theorem is not strictly true, though the discrepancy is too small to be detected in right-angled triangles constructed on this earth. Euclidean theorems are only strictly true in a space *as defined by* Euclid's axioms, and this happens to be a theoretical and artificial space. It has to be appreciated that only in so far as they are used within the constructed and artifical system are the laws of mathematics (arithemetic and geometry) certainly and indubitably true.

It follows from the definitions of '2', '+', '=', '4' and '5' that '2 + 2 = 4' is necessarily true and that '2 + 2 = 5' is necessarily not true. The latter proposition does not make sense; it is not so much false as meaningless. While mathematics is indeed applied to the empirical world we must make no mistake, that it is a truth of *experience* that, say, two beans taken with another two beans are found to yield four beans. To say that two beans taken with another two beans yielded five beans would be to make a false statement, not a meaningless statement. Indeed, the statement *might* be true in that we *found* five beans after we thought we had taken two and then another two: we might have accidentally picked up an extra bean or there might have been one there originally. This may seem to be quibbling but let us consider another case, the addition of two pints (or two litres) of water to two pints (or two litres) of alcohol. We do *not* get four pints (or four litres) of liquid; this is a matter of sense experience, and in no way refutes the mathematical proposition '2 + 2 = 4'. Thus, although mathematics may and often does guide us to a result which can be applied in the empirical world, and which is confirmed by sense experience, we can only rely on a mathematical proposition being indubitably true when it is applied within its own constructed system. When we apply mathematics to the world of sense we cannot be absolutely sure that it will guide us to a result which is in accord with experience. We are confident of the truth of those mathematical propositions which we have arrived at by careful reasoning, because they are *not* empirical propositions; their truth depends solely on the definitions of the terms and the logical relations between the terms and is independent of sense experience.

(ii) Tautologies, Analytic and Synthetic Propositions

A tautology is a self-evident truth and at its simplest it is a statement of equality: for example, '2 = 2' is a tautology, 'A rose is a rose' is a tautology. The truth of such a proposition can be self-evident if we knew the meaning or definitions of the terms. Hence '2 + 2 = 4' is a tautology for most adults, but not for the child learning to count. Similarly 'A bachelor is an unmarried man' is a tautology for those who speak English but not necessarily for a Frenchman. Tautologies may be useless to the man who recognises them as tautologies (though even for him they can act as useful reminders), but they are helpful to others in that they show the meaning of words and implications of definitions. In this last capacity we all find them useful. All deductively logical arguments are tautologies, for the conclusion *must* follow from the premises (see chapter 1, section i), but, as explained in section i, such tautologies are invaluable in revealing the implications of the premises. Similarly the most advanced mathematical theorems are generally tautologous conclusions arising from the definition of number and the simple operations such as 'add', 'subtract', 'differentiate' etc. To a powerful mind these theorems would relate to the basic definitions as obviously as does '2 + 2 = 4', or even '2 = 2'. (Assuming a denary system, '2 + 2 = 11' would be a tautology in a tenary system.)

Because we cannot see all the implications of our definitions so easily, there are many propositions in logic and in mathematics which do not appear as tautologies to us and which therefore give us knowledge and insight into the mathematical and/or logical system which we have constructed. Such propositions, which include obvious tautologies, are called *analytic* propositions. Again, to a powerful mind, truths arrived at by logical deduction, even a very long and complicated process of reasoning, could appear as self-evident truths, self-evident consequences of the premises. Thus we can say that, at bottom, most mathematical truths (see footnote on p. 1) and correctly deduced logical conclusions are tautologies in relation to definitions, axioms and premises, and thus *in a sense* all analytic propositions are tautologies.

However, analytic propositions are by no means always self-evident for us and, because they do give us knowledge and insight, we may be misled into believing that they are conveying real information about the empirical world. Indeed there are some philosophers who think there can be no clear distinction between analytic propositions and those giving us information about the empirical world. We can ignore this dispute here (but see references to Quine and to Grice and Strawson on p. 139). We may take it that analytic propositions, which include mathematical truths, are certainly true, but they do not tell us anything about the empirical world, they only reveal connections *within* a given mathematical or logical system. When analytic propositions appear to give us information about the world, they are either giving us insight into our system, or, like the mathematical propositions discussed above, they are no longer analytic propositions. In so far as they apply to the world they lose their certainty.

All propositions about the properties and behaviour of objects in the empirical world, whether they be statements about particular objects, or generalisations about many objects, are called *synthetic propositions*. Only synthetic propositions can give us knowledge of the empirical world, as opposed to giving us understanding and insight into constructed systems. But we have to accept that no synthetic proposition can have the logical certainty that analytic propositions have. To deny that a synthetic proposition is true, for example, to say 'It is not the case that two beans and two beans make four beans' or 'It is not the case that all crows are black', may be to make a false statement, but it is not to make a meaningless statement. All our particular descriptions and all our generalisations about the empirical world can only have a certain probability of being true; there is always a *logical possibility* that they are false.

Particular descriptions which are direct descriptions of something observed, for example, 'This ball is red', are synthetic propositions which come as near to being certainly true as we can expect. But even in such cases we must allow for the possibility of mistake. Certainly when we come to consider generalisations we must always allow for the possibility that they are false. This is partly a matter of considering the *logical possibility* of falsity; it is logically possible that 'All men are mortal' is false. But along with this there is the practical possibility that some essential positive analogy has been disregarded. This is a practical limitation on the reliability of all synthetic or empirical generalisations, be they common-sense generalisations or scientific laws, be they simple qualitative relations between properties or more complex quantitative relations. The limitation applies as much to generalisations which assert that a certain proportion of cases have a given property, for example, '10 per cent of the patients having babies die of puerperal fever', as to generalisations which assert that all cases have a certain property, for example, 'All crows are black.' These latter generalisations may be called *universal generalisations*, whereas the former are called *statistical generalisations*. It is the practical limitation on the reliability of empirical generalisations (statistical and universal) which are of interest to the scientist.

But there is another more fundamental limitation on the reliability of empirical generalisations. It applies equally to statistical and to universal empirical generalisations; the two types of generalisation can, in this context, be treated together. This limitation arises from the fact that inference is made from observed cases to unobserved cases. By deductive logic it is impossible to justify ampliative inference from certain particulars to other particulars (eductions) and *a fortiori* it is impossible to justify ampliative inference from certain particulars to an indefinitely large number of other particulars (inductions). Inductive generalisations do describe the observed cases, but they apply also to unobserved cases in the past and present and to all future cases, whether they shall be observed or not. This cannot be justified by deductive logic.

(iii) Hume's Problem

The problem of justifying induction, or rather ampliative inference in general, was first explicitly raised by David Hume (1711–76), though earlier writers, Bishop George Berkeley (1685–1753) and John Locke (1632–1704), had indirectly acknowledged it. They had appreciated that reasoning from cause to effect, say a moving ball striking another ball and 'causing' the second ball to move, was not a matter of logical deduction, that is, that there was no *logical* connection between cause and effect. But they did not appreciate, as Hume did, that if there is no logical connection between cause and effect then such a relationship cannot be used to justify generalisations implying a causal relation, for instance, such a generalisation as 'A moving ball will *cause* an equal-sized ball to move if it should strike it.'

This problem of justification has not been solved, and it will be shown that it cannot be solved so as to satisfy the demands of deductive logic. Nevertheless it is worth considering some of the proposed solutions, partly because the attempts to solve the problem will help us to appreciate the nature of the problem itself, and this is quite difficult, and partly because they throw light on aspects of the important *practical* problem, of finding the essential positive analogy, which was discussed in the previous section. This latter problem is less important to philosophers than is the problem raised by Hume, but it is of very great importance to scientists. Scientists are content to ignore Hume's problem, but they cannot ignore the practical problem.

Because of our animal faith in order and regularity it is extremely difficult to appreciate the nature of the basic problem which Hume raised, and many so-called solutions appear to be solutions only because Hume's problem has not been understood and therefore has not been faced. Hume pointed out that just because a certain empirical generalisation had been shown to be true in the past, there was no logical reason to expect that it would continue to be true, *even if* all the circumstances (apart from time) remained the same. For example, though it has been observed that, without exception, fire produces heat when it burns, there is no logical reason to justify the inference that the next fire will have the same effect. As mentioned above, Berkeley and others had pointed out that there was no logical reason why fire should *cause* heat, but they had failed to carry through the implications of this, that is, why should we rely on it giving us heat? Again, said Hume, though it has been observed without exception that bread is a nourishing food, there is no *logical* reason for believing that the next piece of bread which is eaten will be any more nourishing than a piece of stone. In general, said Hume, we have no logical reason for believing that the future will resemble the past.

Of course this argument seems absurd at first; we seem to *know* that fire will burn and we would certainly not put our hand in the flame to test this; we seem to *know* that bread is, and will continue to be, a nourishing food. Hume would agree; but such appeals as to how we feel entirely miss the point of Hume's argument. We would say that our justification for feeling so certain that fire burns and will burn, and that bread nourishes and will nourish, is that we and everyone else we have met or heard of has experienced these effects regularly and repeatedly and without exception. We have also found that other things – friction, electricity, light – regularly and repeatedly produce heat and that other materials – eggs, milk, meat etc – are regularly and repeatedly nourishing. Our confidence in the generalisations 'Fire burns' and 'Bread nourishes' arises entirely by reason of the animal faith which we have in order and regularity, so that we believe that the future *will* resemble the past. But *this* is the very thing we need to justify. We cannot use an argument which involves our *assuming* that the future will resemble the past to justify a conclusion that the future *will* resemble the past.

It may be said that *in the past*, the then future was shown to resemble the even more remote past. But this is no more than to say that *in the past* fire which we were about to light and bread which we were about to eat was eventually shown to warm us and to nourish us, that is, that *in the past* fire burned and bread nourished us. This is not in dispute, but it gives us no logical reason to justify the belief that fire *will* burn and bread *will* nourish, that is, that the course of events in the future will resemble the course of events in the past.

It is important to note that Hume questioned even the right to assert that there was a probability of empirical generalisations being true in the future. We cannot, by deductive logic, show that there is even a remote chance of the generalisations being true. In chapter 7 the probability of a given generalisation being true is discussed, but this is in the context of *practical* probability – a deliberation as to the likelihood of all the essential positive analogy being known and recognised. In the methodology of natural science this probability is of the greatest importance, but when we are considering Hume's problem it is irrelevant.

There have been many attempts to answer Hume. Hume himself regarded the problem as insoluble but gave an account of how our confidence in the generalisations of everyday life and of science arose. He said that because certain events had been observed to be invariably associated, the mind was led to expect regular association in the future, and so we would expect that fire would always burn, bread would always nourish and so on. This is nothing more than an assertion that we have animal faith. Others have tried to provide more than a psychological explanation of the trust we have in the truth of our empirical generalisations.

(iv) Attempts to Answer Hume: (a) Kant

One of the earliest and one of the most profound attempts to show that induction could lead us to certain knowledge, and this included certain scientific knowledge, was made by the German philosopher Immanuel Kant (1724–1804). Kant was especially concerned to justify scientific knowledge. He believed that the theorems of Euclidean geometry were indubitably true of the world of phenomena and that so also were the laws of Newtonian mechanics. He appreciated that appeals to experience could not justify induction, for they must rely on the future being like the past, and so he sought to establish the truth of some empirical propositions, which were of course synthetic propositions, on the basis of their being known *a priori*, that is, before experience and therefore independently of experience. How could this be?

Kant was the first to suggest what has already been referred to in chapter 1, the view that perception is not a passive process, *even* at the most simple level. Conscious appreciation of the most simple sensations must involve some inner activity of the mind. Kant said that, in order to have *any* conscious experience sensations must be structured in accordance with *a priori* intuitions of space and time. These intuitions were *a priori* because they were in the mind *before* and therefore independently of experience. It was only because we had these intuitions that we could *consciously* appreciate our sensations, even in a subjective sense. Such experience, that is, of subjective sensations. Kant called representations. But by virtue of the intuitions of space and time alone only *subjective* sensations, that is, only representations would be possible – the representations would not be referred to anything outside ourselves. In order to have *objective* experience of an external world, as opposed to a rhapsody of perceptions, our representations had themselves to be structured in accordance with *a priori* Concepts. Like the *a priori* intuitions of space and time, these Concepts were in the mind *before* experience and were therefore independent of experience.

So Kant held that we could only know the empirical world as something interpreted in accordance with 'rules' which were innate in our minds. He thought that ultimate reality, that which he called 'things-in-themselves' or *noumena*, could never be known. We could only know noumena as interpreted by our *a priori* intuitions and Concepts: these interpretations gave us *phenomena*. Empirical science, which sought knowledge of the world of sense, sought knowledge not of ultimate reality, but of phenomena. But in so far as it did deal only with phenomena, the findings of empirical science must be indubitably true. Phenomena *had* to behave in accordance with the established laws of Newton because these laws were built into our *a priori* Concepts; they constituted some of the rules by which we structured experience. We could not know phenomena behaving in any other way.

One of the *a priori* Concepts was the Concept of necessary causal connection. Kant's argument for there being this particular *a priori* Concept rested on the supposition that we could only know an objective, as opposed to a subjective, ordering of events in time if there was an *a priori* Concept of causality. For instance, he said, we can look at the various parts of a house in any order we choose: our experiences, or rather the order of our experiences, will depend entirely on ourselves and need not relate to the order of the experiences of others. But when we watch a boat floating downstream the order of our experiences is not dependent on ourselves and cannot be reversed. It is only because we have such irreversible series of sensations that there is the possibility of our appreciating *objective* time, so that we can talk about 'before' and 'after' and agree with others. The fact that the experiences are irreversible, or rather that the irreversibility of their order is appreciated, is due to our possessing an *a priori* Concept of objective causality, of causes outside ourselves. By showing that the Concept of causality was independent of experience, Kant could use it as an independent justification of causal relations. He could, he thought, thus justify induction; he could appeal to a causal principle which was independent of experience and therefore independent of any argument which assumed that the future must resemble the past.

But there are two great objections to Kant's view, or rather to his proposed solution of Hume's problem. Kant appealed to the fact that we could have intersubjective agreement about events in time, and this could only be so if we possessed an *a priori* Concept of cause. However, all we know is that *hitherto* intersubjective agreement about time has been possible; we have no logical reason for expecting our coming sensations to be the same. Therefore objective time, and the possibility of agreeing with others, is a matter of fact only up to this present moment. Our experience does not tell us about time in general, but only about time up to the present moment. Moreover, even if we could accept that there was a general *a priori* causal principle, that is, that the notion of causal relation was independent of experience, this still would not help us to establish the truth of any particular causal relation. We could not be sure that any particular effect was necessarily (*logically* necessarily) due to a certain cause. Kant did not seem to have appreciated this distinction.

For example, Kant held that we *had* to think of space and force as described by Euclid and by Newton. He said that our view of space as Euclidean space and our view of force as Newtonian force was independent of experience. Phenomena *had* to behave in accordance with the theorems of Euclidean geometry and Newtonian mechanics. Now it has been shown that phenomena do not behave in this way and that we do not *have* to think of space as Euclidean space or of action between bodies in terms of Newtonian mechanics. Therefore, even if we accept that the concept of necessary causal connection is needed for intersubjective agreement about time (and as has been shown this involves an inductive assumption that such agreement will continue), this still does not help, in any particular case, to justify an inductive generalisation that a given particular event will invariably be succeeded by some other given event, or that one particular property, or group of properties, will invariably accompany some other particular property.

Kant's answer to Hume's problem is to assert that our minds are so constructed that we cannot have any objective experience without certain concepts which structure our experience in a certain way. The concepts can therefore justify certain inductive inferences by which we arrive at generalisations about phenomena. But quite apart from the inductive assumption that objective knowledge will continue to be possible, we must also acknowledge that Kant's account cannot justify any particular induction, and that therefore it cannot be used to show that any particular relation between phenomena (and this includes all scientific laws) is necessarily true. Thus Kant did not show that any scientific knowledge was indubitably certain knowledge.

(v) Attempts to Answer Hume: (b) Mill and Keynes

In his work on inductive inference, John Stuart Mill (1806–73) tried to justify induction by postulating the law that every event must have a cause as a fundamental law. This was the Law of Universal Causation. Along with this was the law that like causes produced like effects. This law could be trusted, said Mill, because in all our experience it was never refuted. Therefore we could be confident that, within the confines of the space we could observe and in the time during which we had evidence of events, this law would not be refuted. We could be sure that every event had a cause and that like causes produced like effects. (For further discussion of Mill's work on induction, see chapter 7, section iv.)

However the fallacy in this argument is plain: we have no experience of the future and hence we can have no assurance that the Law of Universal Causation will hold in the future. We cannot know that, in the future, every event must have a cause, and we can be even less certain that a given event (a cause) will be followed by the event (the effect) which followed it in the past.

In any case, as Mill's own writings show, many experiments are needed to show that a given event C is a necessary or sufficient cause of another event E. (See also chapter 7, section iii.) In our experimental investigations we show that a class of experiments in which C-type events occur also contain the occurrence of E-type events. To say that C causes E is a short way of talking about classes of events resembling Cs causing classes of events resembling Es. We cannot appeal to some causal essence or special relation between C and E because on each occasion the Cs and Es must be slightly different. Hence we do not even have experience to justify the assertion that like causes produce like effects, except in the very general way, namely, that a member of the class of Cs is followed by a member of the class of Es. This does not give us a principle of causal essence by which to justify an induction.

Another solution to Hume's problem was proposed by John Maynard Keynes (1883–1946). He suggested a Principle of Uniformity of Nature, which was that *mere* position in time and space could not affect other properties of objects or other characteristics of events. If this principle were assumed to be true then the fact that an event was in the future would not affect its character and hence it would be possible to justify an induction by reference to events in the past. This is an appealing suggestion, for we certainly do feel intuitively that *mere* position in time and *mere* position in space cannot affect objects and events. But there is an enormous practical objection to this Principle, namely, that no object and event can differ from another *merely* by virtue of its position in time and/or space. Any change in these must also effect the *relationship* of the object and event with an indefinitely large number of other objects and events: the relationship with every other object on this earth, also the heavenly bodies, the sun, moon, stars, planets etc. We do not have to be astrologers to regard these as perhaps having some effect. For instance, Olympic records in Mexico were thought to be more easily attainable because the height of the stadium above sea-level was sufficient to reduce materially the value of the gravitational force, and thus to reduce the force, and therefore the muscular effort, an athlete would require. There was a counteracting effect in that the reduced atmospheric pressure meant that there was less oxygen inhaled; but this was thought not to be so important since most of the competitors had the opportunity to acclimatise themselves to the height and had enough *time* to produce more red blood corpuscles. A change in the place or time of an event may make a great difference because it is never possible to say that the change was *merely* in the place or in the time.

But to affirm that mere position in time and space are irrelevant is to propose an answer to Hume's problem which is unsatisfactory for another reason: there is no justification for this principle save a rather dubiously reliable experience. Experience, even if absolutely reliable, can be experience of observed events only and cannot be used to justify induction, for, as we have seen, arguments from experience assume the very principle which they are trying to justify.

Another solution of the problem was suggested by Keynes: the Principle of Limited Independent Variety. This proposed solution was elaborated by the Cambridge philosopher C. D. Broad (1887–1972). Broad postulated that there was only a relatively limited number of *kinds* of object in the empirical world, and that what we call material objects show a certain degree of permanence or stability. Therefore, given some of the properties or characteristics of an object, others could be inferred with near certainty because the number of *kinds* of object were limited. It will be seen that this principle also accounts for what was pointed out as being the rather surprising success of arguments from analogy (discussed in chapter 2, section i). Broad pointed out that there were only about 100 known elements and that the number of compounds derived from them, though very great, was still surprisingly small compared to the mathematical possibilities. Again the number of different kinds of living creature was surprisingly small. Objects of similar kind and living things of similar kind are not *identical*, but they show enough similarity to be grouped into kinds with no great difficulty. Broad argued that there was at least some probability that this limitation on the number of kinds was not restricted to the one small part of the universe which we happened to know. If there was only a small probability that the Principle of Limited Independent Variety were true, then every observation in conformity with the Principle would increase this probability (see chapter 8) and so make it more nearly certain. The Principle of Limited Independent Variety would thus provide an independent justification of induction.

Now it is no denial of the Principle to say that we have no logical reason to believe that it is even remotely probable that it will hold in the future. It is experience which has given us confidence that it may have been true and is true. We rely on past and present knowledge. This means that the Principle is itself justified, or given finite probability in virtue of induction, therefore it cannot be used to support or to justify induction.

(vi) The Hopelessness of Logical Justification of Induction

We cannot hope to justify induction; it is logically impossible to do so. G. H. von Wright says that the question of justification can be rephrased 'Given that in present experience all As are Bs, can we guarantee that an unknown instance of A will also have the property B – taking it that A and B are different (that is, logically unrelated) properties?' (*The Logical Problems of Induction*.)

According to von Wright this question involves a contradiction and must be answered by saying 'No', or, better still, by saying that the question is meaningless. For, if A and B are logically unrelated properties then the presence of A does *not*, by logical definition, entail the presence of B and therefore we cannot *guarantee* that the next unknown A will also be a B. If we could *guarantee* this, then A would be logically related to B and our question has ruled out this possibility –

future As must be unknown as regards their possession of property B.

An example will help to make this matter of logical relations clear. If we affirm that 'All samples of chlorine gas are green', then, if greenness is logically related to chlorine gas it would follow that a sample of gas which was *not* green could not be chlorine gas, even if it had all the other properties of chlorine gas. But if greenness is *not* logically related to chlorine gas then a gas like chlorine in every respect but colour could also be called chlorine. Our question 'Given that in present experience all samples of chlorine gas are green, can we guarantee that an unknown instance of chlorine gas will always be green – taking it that chlorine gas samples and greenness are different (that is, logically unrelated) properties?' *requires* there to be a logical possibility that a sample of chlorine gas might not be green.

It might be objected that when we speak of the sample of chlorine gas (an instance of A) as being *unknown*, we mean that it has not yet been observed, so that we have no reason based on observation to say that it is green (possesses the property B). If we wish to justify induction we must merely find some reason, other than observation, by which we could guarantee that it would be green (have property B). But the question insists that the reason must be of a kind such that we are eventually *bound to* observe the sample of chlorine gas as green (we must guarantee that A will be B).* We must guarantee that the sample of chlorine will be green. This leads us back to the contradiction – for if there is to be a *guarantee*, the gas will *not* be unknown as far as its possession of the property of greenness goes. (A will not be unknown as far as its possession of B is concerned.) Yet the question requires that it be unknown in this respect. Hence there is a contradiction contained in it and it is meaningless; or at the very best all we can answer is 'No'.

(vii) Popper's Alternative: The Hypothetico-Deductive Method

A different kind of answer to Hume's problem is suggested by

---

* The argument was based on a question involving a universal proposition, but it can be applied equally well to a question involving a statistical proposition: 'Given that in present experience x per cent of As are Bs can we guarantee that among unknown As, x per cent will have the property B – taking it that A and B are different (that is, logically unrelated) properties?'

Karl Popper. He denies that induction plays any part in giving us knowledge of the empirical world. He suggests that on the basis of our expectation of order, we make hypotheses or tentative conjectures about the nature of the world. Popper's view is different from that of Kant, for Kant thought that our expectations (expressed as our having objective experience) *had* to be fulfilled; that phenomena *had* to conform to our concepts for us to know them. Popper grants that the *expectation* of order is *a priori*, that is, before experience and therefore independent of experience, but does not affirm that in any given case that expectation will be fulfilled. In other words we cannot rely on there being an order which we expect. Popper emphasises that our conjectures and hypotheses can never be *certainly* true; we must be content with hypotheses of which we can, at best, say that they have not been refuted by experience.

For, having formulated a hypothesis, albeit perhaps a very tentative hypothesis, propositions describing certain consequences may be logically deduced, and these consequences must be such that they can be directly observed.* It is only if propositions describing directly observable consequences can be deduced that the hypothesis can be called a scientific hypothesis and therefore be one which gives scientific knowledge of the empirical world. (Popper does not think that hypotheses with no observable consequences, that is, metaphysical hypotheses, should be dismissed by scientists, for he appreciates that metaphysical speculation may kindle the imagination and may eventually lead to scientific hypotheses.) However, assuming that the hypothesis does have observable consequences, then, if observations support these, the hypothesis is said to be *corroborated*. Thus, says Popper, in gaining knowledge of the world, we do *not* perform an induction, we do *not* generalise from particular instances. On the contrary, we use our imagination, we speculate as to what might be the case, and then we see whether our conjectures will stand the test of experience.

This account of scientific discovery is an account of the hypothetico-deductive method, and there is no doubt that it is a good account of how many discoveries, perhaps all discoveries, are made and how scientific knowledge increases. But it is incorrect to say that

---

* To deduce propositions describing an observable event from a theory which consists of propositions about non-observables, there must be minor premises specifying the link between observables and non-observables, and also specifying particular conditions. See chapters 5 and 6.

induction is not involved in any way. The mechanism as to *how* the hypothesis first arises may well involve induction, for the very notion of an expectation of order points to an inductive generalising from experience. Moreover the fact that imaginative and fruitful hypotheses come from those who have considerable experience and knowledge of the subject strongly suggests that there is some unconscious process, analogous to our early spontaneous inductions, at work.

Whether the production of an explanatory hypothesis involves induction is perhaps a matter for psychologists rather than for philosophers (and Popper himself says this), but at least induction as the underlying process cannot be ruled out. For instance, Semmelweiss's conjectures as to the factors which increased the death rate in his First Division could only be made because he had a great deal of experience; to produce a possible explanatory hypothesis requires experience. We may say that today doctors would at once have seen what was the probable cause of the high death rate in Semmelweiss's First Division because they have far more experience, and therefore knowledge, of the causes of infection than had Semmelweiss. Conversely, an observer with less experience and knowledge than Semmelweiss would have been unlikely to have made use of the clue of the colleague's death.

To produce a hypothesis which is precise requires experience. An inexperienced investigator into Semmelweiss's problem might have suggested that the high death rate in the First Division was due to the *presence* of medical students rather than mid-wife nuns. Removal of the medical students (and their replacement by nuns) would indeed have lowered the death rate and the hypothesis would have been confirmed. But such a hypothesis is too vague; it has not indicated the relevant factor about the medical students. It would have been much the same to suggest that the First Division be closed. The hypothesis is not providing a genuine scientific explanation, for to say merely that the students, *as students*, raised the death rate is to make a conjecture which is too vague to be useful.

However, even if we dismiss the claim that there is induction in arriving at an explanatory hypothesis as unproven, we have not avoided induction in the application of the hypothetico-deductive method. This is because we rely on corroborating and refuting observations. We assume that a particular corroborating observation will continue to corroborate and that likewise a refuting observation will continue to refute. Both these assumptions involve acceptance of induction;

they involve our accepting that the future will resemble the present and the past.

To take an example – if we maintain that Semmelweiss's hypothesis that cadaveric matter increased the incidence of puerperal fever was arrived at as a result of imaginative insight, and that there was no induction involved, we have not thereby shown that his hypothesis is established or corroborated independently of induction. Semmelweiss deduced that if his students washed their hands in chloride of lime, then the incidence of fever would be decreased because the cadaveric matter would be destroyed. But to conclude that washing the hands in chloride of lime would be *consistently* effective in reducing the incidence of the disease in these circumstances is itself an induction.

We must also consider the second point, that of refutation. Admittedly if the washing of the hands in chloride of lime had had no effect on the death rate, then Semmelweiss's hypothesis, as applied to that time and place, that is, in 1847 in his hospital in Vienna, would have been conclusively falsified. But it would be an induction to assert that it would be false elsewhere and at other times. This point may be illustrated by taking a hypothesis which Semmelweiss *did* regard as having been falsified: the hypothesis that the dramatic arrival of the priest frightened the patients so much that they became more susceptible to puerperal fever. The fact that when the priest came unobtrusively to the dying there was no alteration in the death rate showed Semmelweiss that the hypothesis was false. But it was an inductive generalisation to conclude that the mode of the priest's arrival would continue to have no effect on the death rate from puerperal fever. Hence, though Popper's account of discovery via hypothesis and test does describe scientific procedure, it does not thereby dispense with the necessity for induction. It is likely that science progresses by the hypothetico-deductive method, but we cannot therefore set Hume's problem aside as being irrelevant.

(viii)   A Reason for Trusting Induction

The most successful attempt to deal with the problem posed by the hope of justifying induction was made by – Reichenbach (1891–1953)*, a German philosopher of science who emigrated to the United States and published a work called *Experience and Prediction* in 1938.

* Reichenbach's work had been anticipated by C. S. Pierce. See reference in A. J. Ayer, *The Origins of Pragmatism*, p. 91.

We do not, Reichenbach said, allot a probability of truth to an inductive generalisation *before* observation and experimentation, but only when experience has shown us that a certain event has always occurred under certain conditions (or has occurred in some definite proportion of instances). Now, said Reichenbach, if there is indeed regularity and uniformity in the sequence of events, we can justifiably predict that the particular event will occur invariably (or in an established proportion of cases) when the prior conditions are those required. We cannot claim that an inductive inference is an indubitably true statement, but truth, in these circumstances, is an idealisation. What we can say is that an inductive inference gives us the best wager. It is the best wager because it is only if inductive procedure is applicable, that is, if there is indeed uniformity in events, that there is even a possibility of making a prediction as to events in the future.

In other words, if it is possible to make true empirical generalisations and to arrive at true scientific laws, then inductive inference must be valid. We must admit that inductive procedure, that is, generalising from past experience, is sufficient for the possibility of success only if there is uniformity in nature, and if the future does resemble the past in the relevant respect. We must admit that we do not and cannot *know* whether the procedure is sufficient, and therefore we can never claim that we are certain to be successful.

Hume believed that we could not justify inductive inference because we could not *know* whether we should be successful. But it is better to consider the problem differently: we can affirm that it would not be possible to apply inductive methods and make empirical generalisations if we knew that these generalisations were likely to be false. On these lines it is possible for us to justify choosing the simplest generalisation, and if we can establish a mathematical relation, of choosing the simplest equation which is compatible with the facts observed. It is not merely economy of intellectual effort, nor the desire for simplicity on aesthetic grounds or grounds of mathematical 'elegance'. Simplicity is a relative matter, and indeed a given curve may be simple if referred to one set of axes and complex if referred to another. It is rather that it has been found that a curve, simple at least in respect to one set of axes, does indeed represent the most effective scientific laws. We may connect points by straight lines, and, as we accumulate more points, each corresponding to another observation, we find from experience that they lead to a smooth curve. We cannot make any claims for the future except to say that connecting points by straight lines will eventually lead to a smooth curve, *if* there is any such curve at all.

We have to concede that we cannot positively justify induction, but we can say that it has not been shown to be unsuccessful: a great many of our empirical generalisations and laws are found to be reliable. There is therefore no reason for us to distrust inductive inference. We rely on animal faith to give us a positive trust in induction; we rely on reason to show that we have no evidence to distrust induction.

Philosophically, it is unsatisfactory not to have a more positive justification of inductive inference, but the position is not unsatisfactory for the scientist. Having accepted that there is no reason why he should *not* attempt to generalise, he can study the various practical ways by which he can ensure that he has found all the essential positive analogies between his instances, and so increase the probability that his empirical generalisations are true, and that he has some generalised knowledge of the world of sense. He seeks to make his generalisations and laws more reliable wagers.

As scientists or philosophers of science we are concerned with the ways in which *practical* limitations on the truth of inductive generalisations may be removed, and not with the *validity* of induction as a mode of inference. We assume that induction is possible, that inductive inference is permitted inference, and we can at least assert that it has not been shown to yield consistently unacceptable results.

(ix) The New Riddle of Induction

A rather different approach to the problem of justification has been raised by Nelson Goodman. He thinks that the classical 'problem' can be dismissed but that it is replaced by another problem.

He affirms Hume's view that there cannot be necessary connections between matters of fact and supports Hume's opinion that our belief in necessary connection is due to custom and habit. He says the criticism of Hume's opinion is based on the fact that his explanation only shows how the belief in necessary connection *comes about* and *not* how it is *justified*. But Goodman holds that the problem of the justification of induction cannot be dissociated from the problem of describing how it comes about.

Goodman reminds us that *deductive* inferences are regarded as valid or justified if they are in accord with certain rules of inference which *we have come to regard* as having some sort of objective validity. But, in fact, we use them because they work:

> Principles of deductive inference are justified by their conformity with accepted deductive practice. Their validity depends upon accordance with the particular deductive inferences' we actually make and sanction. If a rule yields inacceptable inferences, we drop it as invalid. Justification of general rules thus derives from judgements rejecting or accepting particular deductive inferences.

Goodman appreciates that this is, in a sense, a circular argument: rules are justified because they conform to valid inferences, and inferences are held to be valid because they conform to accepted rules. But he affirms that it is not a 'vicious' circle for it is a question of bringing rules and inferences to agree in that:

> a rule is amended if it yields an inference we are unwilling to accept; an inference is rejected if it violates a rule we are unwilling to amend.

It must be admitted that amendment of deductive rules may be possible but, in actual practice it is almost inconceivable that it is not the resulting *inference* which would be suspect. However, Goodman's point is allowable in principle. It can be argued that the reason *why* the accepted deductive rules of inference seem 'impregnable' is that they have been tried and tested for centuries. What Goodman wishes to emphasise is that they are not absolutely sacrosanct and are not in this way to be set apart from rules for valid *inductive* inference. The latter are also justified by conformity to general rules, and likewise the rules are justified by conformity with particular inductive inferences or the results obtained by using the rules to make predictions. The difference is that the rules are not so firmly established and the predictions cannot be guaranteed to be correct. This fallibility of the predictions is something with which Goodman is not directly concerned. He implies that *if* the valid principles of induction could be found, *then* correct prediction would follow. But, of course if, like deduction, it is a question of bringing rules and inferences into agreement there would always remain the possibility of amendment of the rules.

However, if we accept his argument, we can see that the problem of *justification* of induction can be dismissed. The *new* problem is, for Goodman, 'What *are* the valid principles of inductive inference?'

'What is to be regarded as appropriate confirmation of a law, a generalisation or a theory?' This is what he calls 'The New Riddle of Induction'. This *is* a problem that Hume overlooked. Goodman says:

> The real inadequacy of Hume's account lay not in his descriptive approach but in the imprecision of his description. Regularities in experience, according to him, give rise to habits of expectation; and thus it is predictions conforming to past regularities that are normal or valid. But Hume overlooks the fact that some regularities do and some do not establish such habits; and that predictions based on some regularities are valid while predictions based on other regularities are not.

The examples he gives of these latter regularities do, of course, appear artificial precisely because our intuitive common sense tells us that they are no basis for prediction. For instance, we may have a theory (or law) that all ravens are black. It follows logically (that is, deductively) that non-black things are non-ravens – something we can unreservedly accept. We also know by *experience*, not by logical deduction from the law, that everything that is not a raven is not necessarily non-black, that is, we know of plenty of black things which are not ravens. But of course we also observe many objects which are *not* ravens and also are *not* black, and this *could be* the experiential (inductive) basis for the inference 'Everything that is not a raven is not black'. Of course we do not accept this inference because of our experience of black things which are *not* ravens. The simple example shows clearly that the inductive inference (based on observing non-black things and finding that they are not ravens) to 'Everything that is not a raven is non-black' and the logical consequence 'All black things are ravens', is plainly not acceptable.

Now let us take a less simple case. We may have evidence that certain materials (of different kinds perhaps) are chemical compounds and this confirms a hypothesis that all materials are chemical compounds, but we may also have evidence that certain materials are not chemical compounds and *this* confirms the hypothesis that no materials are chemical compounds. So we arrive at the conjunction that all materials are both chemical compounds and not chemical compounds. Clearly this is absurd. What is wrong is that in formulating the hypotheses we did not consider *all* the evidence, but how do we *know* when we have all the evidence? We must actively seek to falsify a hypothesis and hope that it will resist falsification, but we have no established rules: our methods are *ad hoc*.

Goodman considers another type of example. The fact that a given piece of copper conducts electricity confirms the hypothesis that all copper conducts electricity. But the fact that one or even several men in a room have three sons does not confirm the hypothesis that all the men in the room have three sons – still less that *all* men have three sons. Again, of course, the common-sense counter to this is to appeal to further evidence: to established scientific laws about metals and conductivity on one hand and to known facts about fatherhood on the other. Nevertheless we have to admit that we are introducing evidence which *experience* tells us is relevant. We have no rules.

Thus, although the scientist will work on the assumption that for each *particular* hypothesis he can in *practice* avoid arriving at contradictory propositions, he has to and in fact almost always does, assume that *all* evidence which he regards intuitively as relevant is taken into account. He can never be sure that this is the case. He may by-pass the classical problem of inductive validity but he has the new problem of confirmation. At present he must regard this as a practical problem to be solved *ad hoc* in each case. If this new 'riddle' could be answered we would be more confident of the truth of our generalisations from experience. (See pp. 138–9 for Questions and Further Reading related to this chapter.)

5

Theories and Laws

(i) Characteristics of Scientific Theories

In chapter 4, section vii there was a brief account of the hypothetico-deductive method. The hypothesis, perhaps a very tentative one, is put forward as a way of relating or of explaining certain observed facts. The hypothesis may be in the form of an empirical generalisation whereby observations become more ordered, or it may be in the form of a *theory*, whereby the facts are explained. Generally facts are ordered by empirical generalisations and then explained by theories, but, occasionally, as we shall see, the theory itself leads the scientist to new empirical generalisations, that is, to relations between observed facts which had not been previously appreciated.

The tentative hypothesis which connects known facts is in the form of an empirical generalisation. Examples of such hypotheses are that the pressure of a gas is inversely proportional to its volume, at constant temperature (Boyle's law); that the extension of a wire is proportional to the extending force (Hooke's law); that the distance travelled by a dense body in free fall is proportional to the square of the time of fall (Galileo's law). Confirmation of these hypotheses is obtained by direct observation, that is, by seeking similar facts and observing that the relations suggested by the hypothesis do indeed hold. When conducting such tests it is important to seek a variety of instances, so as to increase the negative analogy (see chapter 2, section iii). Observation is conducted not only to confirm but also to test resistance to falsification.

However, if the tentative hypothesis is in the form of an explanatory theory it will do more than suggest relations between known facts. It will suggest new entities which will be related to the facts to be explained. (The entity may be entirely new, for example, the molecule, or it may be a known effect acting in a new way, for example, the *gravitational* force.) An example of a scientific theory is Newton's theory of gravitational attraction where the new entities are the gravitational forces and the resulting gravitational field. Another example is the kinetic theory of gases where the new entities are the gas molecules whose movements are related to the pressure, volume and temperature of the gas. Hypotheses which are in the form of explanatory theories are thus quite different from hypotheses which are in the form of empirical generalisations, for, since they propose new entities, they lead to the possession of new concepts. We may say that, if the hypothesis is established and accepted, it has *educed* new facts.

Thus the distinction between an empirical generalisation and an empirical theory is that the generalisation relates or classifies facts which are already established, whereas the theory *educes* new facts which themselves become established *as facts* when the theory comes to be accepted. Now it may not be possible to establish the existence of the theoretical entities by direct observation. There are many theories which suggest the existence of entities, atoms, molecules, prehistoric animals etc. which are not directly observable. If the theory is to be ranked as a *scientific theory* it must be possible to relate these entities to observation, so that their existence can be inferred.

To infer the existence of theoretical entities from observation we must be able to take the propositions of the theory, which describe those entities, and logically derive other propositions which will correspond to empirical generalisations. We can then predict that a particular observation can be made (that is, a particular phenomenon can be observed at a given time and place) and we can then make the observation and so confirm (or refute) our prediction. If the observation confirms the prediction then it has given us evidence for the existence of the theoretical entity.

For example, from the propositions of the kinetic theory of gases it is possible to derive a generalisation which corresponds to Boyle's law. We may then arrange an experiment whereby pressure and volume of a gas (at constant temperature) are measured, and the product of the pressure and volume is calculated in each instance. If these products are of the same value, or as near to the same as conditions permit, and theory indicates, then we may say that the theory has been confirmed and that the theoretical entities, the gas molecules, are existent entities – that is, their existence is a fact.

In this particular example, the empirical generalisation (Boyle's law) had been established before the theory was suggested, so that the corroborative evidence was already available. It was only necessary to show that deductions from the propositions of the kinetic theory of gases would lead to a generalisation corresponding to Boyle's law. It was not necessary to perform the experiments, they had already been done, but it is always hoped that a theory designed to explain one generalisation may lead the scientist to another generalisation, which it will also explain.* The other generalisation may have been established already, by direct observation, or it may be quite new. In the latter case the scientist must make new observations (and experiments) to corroborate the new generalisation.

For example, Newton's theory of gravitational attraction was devised to explain the empirical generalisations about the motions of the planets which were known as Kepler's laws. But Newton's theory also explains Galileo's law relating to the free fall of objects near to the earth; in other words it is found that Galileo's law can be deduced from the propositions of Newton's theory. To take an example of a theory which led scientists to a completely new observation, we may consider the theory of the circulation of the blood advanced by the English physician William Harvey (1578–1657). From the propositions of the theory we can deduce that there must be some physical connection between arteries and veins in the body. After Harvey's death, when microscopes had been invented, search for such a connection revealed the capillary blood vessels.

It is to be emphasised that a theory cannot be regarded as a *scientific* theory unless it can be related to what can be observed. For example, as it was first formulated, the atomic theory of matter was a scientific theory. It was possible to account for such observed facts as the wearing away of rocks and stones by water, or of a metal ring on the finger, by describing the separation of atoms too minute to be sensed. In other words, it was possible to deduce propositions from the propositions of the theory which corresponded to generalisations based on what could be directly observed. But, as the theory was developed in

* When Maxwell developed the kinetic theory of gases, he was able to show that, if the theory were true, the viscosity of a gas would be independent of its pressure. Observation confirmed the truth of this generalisation and so provided further evidence to support the theory. See also chapter 6.

the Middle Ages, it became unrelated to observation. It was then a theory of *minima*, or the smallest parts of which objects were composed. This theory was not related to any physical or chemical reaction, and therefore could not be confirmed (or refuted) by any chemical or physical reaction, that is, by anything which might be observed. It was then a metaphysical theory, not a scientific theory.

Metaphysical theories are not necessarily to be ignored by the scientist. They have their uses because they can encourage speculative thought. The medieval atomic theory led to the development of a corpuscular theory of matter in the seventeenth century, and this theory did relate to what might be observed. The corpuscular theory itself led to Dalton's atomic theory. Dalton's theory was also a true scientific theory because it could be related to observation. For example, from the theory it was possible to deduce that chemical compounds would have a fixed composition. The generalisation was confirmed by experiment.

There are two outstanding characteristics of any scientific theory. First the theory *explains* observed regularities by relating them to new entities which it educes as existent facts.* Second it must be possible to deduce generalisations from the propositions of the theory which can be used to predict observable events. It is in this way that the new concepts which the theory brings to the scientist are shown to *be* concepts corresponding to facts or empirical concepts.

(ii) Empirical Generalisations and Laws

Empirical generalisations are arrived at by induction from observation. On the basis of observation of particular phenomena and events a tentative hypothesis suggesting some new relationship may be formulated. The tentative hypothesis is tested by reference to further observation. If it is confirmed it will come to be established and accepted as an empirical generalisation.

* We shall be discussing the refutation of theories more fully in the next chapter, but it is necessary to note here that the scientist can never be *absolutely certain* that he has found new facts because he can never be absolutely certain that his theory is true. If observation is found to be in accord with the consequences of a theory, the theory had been confirmed but it has not been *proved* to be true. It is not impossible for a theory to be false and yet to have true consequences. For instance, Ptolemy's theory of the solar system (according to which the sun goes round the earth) is a source of true prediction as to the position of the planets at various times. It may be possible to derive true conclusions from a false theory.

Now it is convenient to distinguish those empirical generalisations which are *mere* empirical generalisations, confirmed by observation, but not supported by any theory, from empirical generalisations which *can* be related to a theory. It is convenient to distinguish generalisations of the type 'All crows are black' from generalisations of the type 'The orbits of the planets are ellipses with the sun in one focus'.

In the latter case the empirical generalisation, which can be directly related to observations, can *also* be deduced from the propositions of a scientific theory. In our particular example, the generalisation 'The orbits of the planets are ellipses with the sun in one focus' can be deduced from the propositions of Newton's theory of gravitational attraction. The original empirical generalisation is thereby explained by the theory, for, if we can deduce a corresponding generalisation from the propositions of the theory, it follows that the generalisation is a logical consequence of the propositions of the theory.

In this text the distinction between mere empirical generalisations and empirical generalisations explained by a theory will be made by calling the latter type of empirical generalisation *laws*.

A law is an empirical generalisation explained by a scientific theory. It does not matter how much a mere empirical generalisation is confirmed by direct observation: it cannot, *for that reason alone*, rank as a law. Thus, 'All men are mortal' is a mere empirical generalisation, even though it has been confirmed an innumerable number of times. (In this context, mortality is not being taken as a defining characteristic of human beings.)

There are also more 'scientific' generalisations, such as 'All Mongol children have a defective chromosome', and 'All electric charges are multiples of the charge on the electron' (this can be compared with Prout's hypothesis that the atoms of the elements were made up of hydrogen atoms which was an empirical generalisation in the early nineteenth century). These generalisations have been well-confirmed by observation and are accepted as true, but they are not scientific *laws* because they cannot be derived from an explanatory theory.

By contrast, Galileo's laws of falling bodies and Kepler's laws of planetary motion can be derived from Newton's theory of gravitational attraction. Boyle's law and Charles's law can be derived from the kinetic theory of gases. Hooke's law can be derived from theories of the molecular structure of solids. Ohm's law can be derived from theories of the behaviour of electrons and ions. The derivation may be relatively simple (as in the case of the derivation of Kepler's laws), or it may involve assumptions of 'ideal' behaviour (as in the case of Boyle's law) or it may involve making quite severe restrictions (as in the case of Hooke's law). But all these generalisations are related, albeit sometimes in a complicated fashion, to explanatory theories. Since the theories are themselves accepted, the generalisations are true laws in the sense that we use the term here.

(iii) Mutual Support for Laws and Theories

We see that laws, though grounded in observation,* must also be supported by theories if they are to be regarded as true scientific laws rather than as mere empirical generalisations. There is a reciprocal support of theories by laws and laws by theories: generalisations derived from the propositions of a theory support empirical generalisations and give them the status of laws, but those same empirical generalisations, which are of course derived from observation, in their turn support the theory.

It might be thought that such a relationship comes dangerously close to a self-contained system – a strong chain with no point of support – for empirical generalisation supports theory, and theory supports empirical generalisation. Particular propositions, derived from either the theory or the empirical generalisation, refer to the same particular observation. This weakness is especially marked if one theory supports just one empirical generalisation and *vice versa*, that is, if only one generalisation, corresponding to an empirical generalisation, can be derived from the theory, so that the theory supports and is supported by one and the same law. A theory of this sort may be

---

* Not all our scientific laws state relations between phenomena which can be directly observed. For instance, Avogadro's law states that equal volumes of gases (at the same temperature and pressure) contain equal numbers of molecules. This is because some scientific theories, such as the kinetic theory of gases, have become so well-established that the entities which they educe are treated as existing in the same way as directly observable entities. Therefore further relations come to be suggested. In this way the concepts of these theoretical entities, the molecules in the above example, are extended. The distinction between a scientific law and theory is *not* that the former is concerned with observable phenomena and the latter is not. It is that a law states a new relation between entities which are *already* educed as facts. By contrast a scientific theory educes *new* facts. We can call Avogadro's law a *law* as opposed to a hypothesis because it can be deduced from the kinetic theory of gases (see previous section).

called an *ad hoc* theory, or, more usually, an *ad hoc* hypothesis, since it is likely to be only tentatively accepted. It is a very weak theory if it can be related to only one empirical generalisation. For instance, Boyle's theory that gases were composed of spring-like particles was an *ad hoc* hypothesis which accounted for the fact that the pressure of a gas was inversely proportional to its volume, but it did not even account for the proviso, that the law held only at constant temperature. It could not account for Charles's law, that the volume of a gas is directly proportional to the temperature (at constant pressure). By contrast, the kinetic theory of gases accounts for both Charles's and Boyle's laws (and for other laws). Similarly, Newton's theory accounts not only for Kepler's laws but also for Galileo's laws. Kepler's laws appear to be entirely unconnected with Galileo's laws, and there is more support for Newton's theory in that it supports and is supported by two apparently widely different sets of laws.

A theory which explains two or more empirical generalisations links those generalisations so that they support each other. Moreover, *as a group*, those generalisations support the theory and give it greater support than would any of them if considered separately and then the sum total of their contribution to confidence were assessed. The whole system is self-contained but it is a much bigger system, and because it is bigger, and *yet* in accordance with observation and internally consistent, there are more reasons for trusting it. It follows that any apparent exception to any one of the laws of the system, which might arise from observation, is very disturbing. For, if the exception is accepted – that is, the relevant observation is confirmed and held not to be mistaken – not only is the law undermined, but the theory itself is attacked and, with it, all the other laws which the theory supports are at least called into question. (The process of refutation of laws and theories is discussed in the next chapter; here we are primarily concerned with the mutual support of theories and laws.)

(iv) Correction of Empirical Generalisations by Theories

We have seen that theories support generalisations based on observation because generalisations *corresponding to* those observations can be derived from theory. But theories also support laws in another way, which, curiously enough, is by correcting them.

Once our scientific laws go beyond the vagueness of common-sense formulation and are stated in the form of a quantitative relationship, they become subject to much more severe test by experiment. But experimental measurements may at first be made with relatively crude instruments, so that any discrepancies between what the law predicts and what is actually observed may well be quite properly ascribed to errors of measurement, that is, to experimental errors. Indeed, as was explained in chapter 3, section v, some initial crudity in measurement is helpful for the scientist, for it enables him to arrive at relatively simple laws, such as Galileo's laws and Boyle's law. (See chapter 3, section v.) Any slight discrepancy between law and observation can be attributed to experimental error.

However, as instruments become more accurate and experimental techniques become more skilful, it may be impossible to accept that discrepancies between law and observation are due to experimental error. The scientist has to conclude that the simple empirical law is not strictly true. It is here that the theory can be helpful; it may indicate why what is observed is not strictly in accord with what the law predicts.

For example, if we take a law such as Galileo's law that the acceleration of a body falling towards the earth is 32 feet per second per second (981 cm per second per second), we find that accurate measurement of bodies falling is not in accordance with the law: the acceleration is slightly less than the law requires and is not absolutely constant. Now Newton's theory states that the attractive force between masses varies as the inverse square of the distance between them, and we would therefore expect that as a body fell, and the distance between its centre of gravity and that of the earth's became less, the attractive force, and therefore the resultant acceleration, would increase. In addition, Newton's theory does not assume any external opposition to the force; but a body falling in air is not falling absolutely freely since it encounters resistance from the air. Therefore the attractive force is being opposed and the resultant acceleration will be less than that acquired in truly free fall. Thus the theory not only tells us that the observations will not be in accordance with the simple law, it shows why this will be so – namely because the varying distance between the earth and the falling body, and the resistance of the air during falling, is not taken into account.

As another example we may consider Boyle's law. Accurate measurements show that pressure and volume of a gas are not exactly inversely proportional to each other at constant temperature.

The kinetic theory of gases indicates that we must allow for the space occupied by the gas molecules when we calculate the volume of the gas, and that we must allow for the attractive force between gas molecules when we calculate the pressure of the gas. Adjustments for these factors leads us to another law, Van der Waal's law, which is found to be in much better accordance with observation – again the theory has indicated why the simple law was not in accordance with observation, and it has also indicated how the simple law may be modified to accord more with observation.

As our measurements become more accurate and more refined we see that our simple laws are not strictly in accordance with observation. It is very great confirmation of our scientific theories (those which explain the simple laws) if generalisations can be directly derived from those theories which do correspond more closely to what is in fact observed with the more accurate measuring instruments. It is even better if the theory can indicate *why* the more simple law is less in accordance with refined observation, that is, why the simple law is no longer adequate.

For example, Galileo's law can be tested by conducting experiments on bodies falling *in vacuo* (there will then be no air resistance) and it is found that the acceleration is much more nearly that required by the simple law. Boyle's law can be tested with gases at very low pressures and relatively high temperatures. The kinetic theory indicates that, under these conditions (when the total volume occupied by the gas is large compared to the volume of the gas molecules, and when the pressure, due to the high velocity of the gas molecules, is great compared to the attractive force between the molecules), Boyle's law will be in much closer agreement with what is observed. This is found to be the case.

(v) Replacement of Theories

Generalisations derived from scientific theories correspond to empirical generalisations, and, as was shown in the previous section, we may find that the generalisations derived from the theory are in closer accordance with what is observed. However, even these generalisations may be found to be slightly inaccurate.

In the previous section it was shown that Newton's theory of gravitational attraction could account for the discrepancies between Galileo's law and what could be observed. But more refined measurement reveals discrepancies in the theory itself. Measurements over very great astronomical distances have revealed anomalies between what Newton's theory predicts and what is in fact observed. Einstein's special Theory of Relativity introduces corrections to Newton's theory.

In general, a new and more comprehensive theory leads to modifications of the theory it replaces. The new theory will account for the anomalies which may have prompted scientists to speculate and to produce the new theory. The anomalies will certainly have made them dissatisfied with the older theory, but it is very rare that a new theory upsets the fundamental principles of the relevant branch of science. When this does happen, as is the case with ideas about mass and momentum in modern physics, it may well be the case that the older theory will still be used in circumstances where it can be applied with reasonable accuracy, that is, where there is reasonable accordance between predictions made with the help of the theory and observation. Thus Newtonian mechanics is still used in engineering, to calculate forces, stresses and strains, in ordinary-sized objects. Quantum mechanics is only used for calculations connected with observations on sub-atomic phenomena. Strictly speaking quantum mechanics applies to all bodies, but the difference in practical results between it and Newtonian mechanics, when applied to macro-objects, is much less than anything that can be detected even with our sensitive instruments. The more complicated calculations involved in applying quantum mechanics are therefore not warranted.

However, it has to be admitted that such theories as the quantum theory and Einstein's Relativity Theories do profoundly affect the scientist's concepts of fundamentals such as mass, momentum, space and time. Whilst holding that most new theories lead only to relatively superficial modifications of our system of scientific knowledge, we must be prepared to concede that some theories, though not having made much practical difference to our everyday calculations or to many scientific experiments, have profoundly altered the scientist's concepts of some very fundamental notions.

(vi) Theories as Descriptions of the World

The fact that scientific theories can modify and correct laws which relate to observables, and can sometimes modify very fundamental concepts, is very strong evidence for regarding such theories as giving descriptions of a reality behind appearances. If they are descriptions *of this sort*, then they can be said to be true theories or false theories. A true theory is one which has been satisfactorily corroborated; we take it to be true if it has been adequately confirmed by being related to observation in the way described in sections ii and iii. When such a true theory comes to be modified by some more comprehensive theory, as when Newton's theory came to be modified by Einstein's theory, the older theory is not rejected as being totally false. It is held that it did not tell the scientist the whole truth, but only part of the truth. Only on the comparatively rare occasions when a theory comes to be completely discarded – as has the theory of Claudius Ptolemy (85–165) concerning the arrangement of the heavenly bodies, or the phlogiston theory of combustion – may theories be said to be completely false. We can be almost certain that none of our present theories gives us the whole truth, but we can hope that they give us at least part of the truth, and that they will come to be modified, as Newton's theory has been modified, rather than be completely rejected as Ptolemy's theory has been.

Now Ptolemy's theory was used for a very long time, and indeed was regarded as true because it did, within the limits of accuracy obtainable at the time, enable the positions of the heavenly bodies to be predicted correctly. But at the end of chapter 4, section ix it was pointed out that though a theory may be a source of true predictions, this cannot be taken as proof that the theory itself is true. We must therefore grant that a theory may be *useful* in this way, whether or not it is true.

There have been many scientists and many philosophers of science who have argued that the question of whether the theory itself is true or false is irrelevant; the only important thing is that the theory should be a source of true laws, of true generalisations about observables. They say that since a theory can never be proved to be true by showing that generalisations derived from it can be in accordance with observations, it is better not to regard it as consisting of the *sort* of propositions which could be true or false. Theories should not be regarded as providing descriptions, they should be regarded merely as sets of propositions which give a convenient or intellectually helpful means of arriving at empirical laws, and of co-ordinating those laws. Theories may, on this view, be said to be useful or useless, but not true or false. Theories may therefore be regarded as *instruments* helping the scientist to arrive at empirical laws; modern proponents of this view are called instrumentalists.

Instrumentalists say that is is best to think of theories as providing rules whereby we can arrive at true laws and make true predictions about observables. The instrumentalist view can be objected to on two main grounds.

Firstly such a view must lead us to make a sharp distinction between *laws* which state relations between observables, and *theories* which state relations between unobservables, and this is very difficult because there are so many entities which are of dubious status or which have been of dubious status. In Harvey's time blood capillaries were not observable, and therefore his theory of the circulation of the blood would not have been taken, by instrumentalists, as a description of what happened, but only as a convenient instrument for co-ordinating the various observed facts about blood in the arteries and veins. But now the capillaries can be seen under a microsope; according to the instrumentalist view, Harvey's theory has changed its nature and has now become a set of laws. It can now be regarded as being true or false rather than as useful or useless. As another example we may take the case of molecules. Today the larger molecules can be 'seen' in outline with the help of the electron microscope. Are molecules now to count as observable phenomena, and are the propositions of the kinetic theory thus to change their status and become laws? It would seem that the nature of a given set of propositions would depend on the advances made in the design of scientific instruments.

A second objection, which is more serious, is that the instrumentalist view completely fails to account for the fact that a theory which may have been arrived at by speculating on possible explanations of an empirical generalisation, can so frequently be found to explain other empirical generalisations. For example, Newton's theory of gravitational attraction explains the elliptical orbits of the planets, but it also explain Galileo's laws. The instrumentalist view also fails to account for the fact that a theory may be elaborated and extended so as to lead the scientist to new laws which were not arrived at by direct observation, but which can be confirmed by direct observation. For example, the electronic theory of valency led to laws about the reactivity of chemical elements which were later confirmed by observation. On an instrumentalist view most theories should be *ad hoc* hypotheses – it should be a matter of most extraordinary coincidence that they should be related to more than one empirical generalisation, and that they should be capable of extension so that new empirical generalisations can be derived from them. The instrumentalist view is methodologically very unhelpful because, if it were believed, scientists would be discouraged from imaginatively developing their theories.

A more sophisticated and more helpful form of instrumentalism has recently been proposed by Laudan. He holds that the primary aim of science is the resolution and clarification of problems, as opposed to the explaining of the natural world. For Laudan, the acid test of any theory is whether it provides satisfactory solutions to problems which are currently considered important. Therefore, when appraising a theory he says that we should ask whether it provides an adequate solution or solutions to significant problems rather than ask whether the theory is 'true' or 'well-confirmed'.

Progress in science is achieved by more effective solving of problems and

> any time we modify a theory or replace it by another theory, that change is progressive if and only if the later version is a more effective problem solver . . . than its predecessor. (L. Laudan, *Progress and its Problems*, (London: 1977) p. 68.)

Laudan suggests that we should distinguish between theories which 'denote a very specific set of related doctrines', for example, Maxwell's theory of electromagnetism or the Freudian theory of the Oedipal complex, from theories which are effectively *sets* of doctrines or assumptions, such as the theory of evolution or the atomic theory. He prefers to call these more global theories 'research traditions'. Research traditions embrace a number of the specific theories of the former kind. The research tradition is fundamentally normative and metaphysical but it can be evaluated because

> a successful research tradition is one which leads, via its component theories, to the adequate solution of an increasing range of empirical and conceptual problems.

Clearly, this view of theories sets aside the question of truth or falsity as irrelevant, but it avoids the two disadvantages of the older form of instrumentalism, namely its introductions of the problem of distinguishing the observable from the unobservable and its failure to account for the heuristic function of theories. This is because the research tradition does generate conceptual problems, and in practice provides a realist picture.

When, for instance, Huygens came to develop a general theory of motion, he found that the only empirically satisfactory theories were those which assumed vacua in nature. Unfortunately Huygens was working squarely within the Cartesian research tradition, a tradition which identified space and matter and thus forbade empty spaces. As Leibniz and others pointed out to Huygens, his theories were running counter to the research tradition which they claimed to instantiate.

And the research tradition is held to *postulate* entities:

> Precisely because they postulate certain types of entities and certain methods for investigating the properties of those entities, research traditions can play a vital heuristic role in the construction of specific scientific theories.

Hence, although Laudan's exposition is fundamentally instrumentalist, he allows that research traditions (comprehensive theories) and their components (more specific theories) can be treated as giving factual descriptions. Moreover it is when so treated that they encourage discovery.

Taking the view that theories describe a reality behind appearances that is, a realist view, there is no difficulty in admitting that the unobservable theoretical entities become observable as instruments and techniques improve – it is what is to be expected. On the realist view there is no difficulty in accounting for a theory being a source of generalisations which correspond to empirical generalisations, and to different empirical generalisations. The reality behind appearances may well embrace two superficially different laws – the theory itself shows how this is so. Lastly, on the realist view the scientist is positively encouraged to extend and develop the theory so that it can lead him not only to discover new empirical laws, but also to a deeper knowledge about the world which he cannot directly observe.

(vii) Theories as Explanations

If we regard theories as giving us potentially true descriptions of a reality behind appearances, we can see how they help in explaining the world, as well as being a source of laws and a means whereby laws are corrected.

By *explaining* we mean more than that the theory shows us laws which follow logically from its premises, though admittedly this is one aspect of explanation. The view that explanation involves *only* the ability to make true predictions is inadequate. Laws alone enable us to predict truly. We can predict the fall of a stone using Galileo's law; we can predict the expansion of a gas at constant temperature using Boyle's law. It is not enough to say that the relevant theories, Newton's theory of gravitational attraction and the kinetic theory of gases, merely support the empirical generalisations and/or offer more accurate predictions. Explanation also involves understanding of the event. The theory of gravitational attraction helps us to understand the falling of a stone, by putting the event into a broader background of events; the kinetic theory likewise helps us to understand the expansion of a gas. Such understanding is only possible if we regard the theory as *describing* what underlies that which we can directly observe.

A theory explains not only by enabling true predictions to be made but also by linking familiar observed events to the less familiar, perhaps very strange, reality behind appearances. The theory enables us to relate the observed to the unobserved and so gain deeper insight into the world around us.

(viii)   The Explanation of Mendeleef's Classification of the Elements

This classification was first proposed by the Russian scientist Mendeleef (1834–1907) in 1869. By that time many elements had been identified and obtained in a reasonable state of purity and many facts were known about the chemical reactivity of the different elements. It had also become possible to determine the atomic weights of most elements with reasonable certainty.* What Mendeleef did was to suggest a method of classifying the elements in such a way that much of this empirical knowledge became ordered and coherent. Moreover, having established his scheme, he was able to make further suggestions as to properties and reactions, and these were then confirmed by observation. The basic empirical generalisation on which he based his

---

* The atomic weight of an element is the ratio of the weight of an atom of the element to the weight of an atom of hydrogen. (There are other ways of defining atomic weights, by relating them to oxygen or carbon, but the simple and original definition may be taken here).

scheme was

> The elements, if arranged according to their atomic weights, show an evident periodicity of properties

and

> The arrangement of the elements in this way corresponds to their valencies.*

Having made his classification he was able to make the following empirical generalisations, all of which were confirmed by observation.

> Elements which are similar as regards their chemical properties have atomic weights which are either of nearly the same value (platinum, iridium, osmium) or which increase regularly (lithium, sodium, potassium, rubidium, caesium).

> The magnitude of the atomic weight determines the character of the element.
> Certain characteristic properties of the elements can be foretold from their atomic weights.
> The discovery of many yet unknown elements may be expected.

Mendeleef showed that the elements could be considered to be in seven main families or *groups*. Examples of Mendeleef's groups are the alkali metals: lithium, sodium, potassium, rubidium, caesium; and the halogens: fluorine, chlorine, bromine and iodine. We need not go into the details of his scheme, but Mendeleef was able to show, from the gradation of properties and the relations between the groups, that there must be certain elements missing from the original table. On the basis of analogy with other relations in the table he predicted the chemical and physical properties of some of these missing elements with astonishing accuracy. Here is his prediction of some of the properties of a missing element, called eka-silicon by Mendeleef, as compared with germanium, which took the place of the hypothetical

---

* The valency of an element is the combining power of the atoms of the element with the atoms of other elements. It may be defined simply as the number of atoms of hydrogen which will combine with or replace one atom of the element.

eka-silicon in the table when it was discovered.

	Eka-silicon	Germanium
Atomic weight	72	72.6
Density	5.5	5.47
Colour	Dirty grey, giving a white powder of oxide on calcination	Greyish white, giving a white powder on calcination
Action of acids and alkalis	Action of acids will be slight, that of alkalis more pronounced	Metal only attacked by very strong acid mixture. Molten alkali oxidises it

These are only some of the predicted and observed properties; Mendeleef predicted many more which were found to be in accordance with what was observed.

Here therefore we have a table based on empirical generalisations which guides us to other empirical generalisations and which is a source of true prediction. Now, if explanation were solely a matter of ability to predict, it could be claimed that the table *explained* the properties of the elements. But on the view of explanation offered in section vii, it does not offer an explanation; it is a basis of prediction only.

Mendeleef's table was not perfect; there were some anomalies in that certain elements, for example, iodine and tellurium, were set in the wrong groups if they were classified according to atomic weight. There was also no satisfactory place for hydrogen in the table. These anomalies were corrected and the classification was *explained* by the modern atomic theory.

The modern atomic theory, which developed along with the electronic theory of valency, suggests a classification of the elements based on the number and arrangement of the electrons around the atomic nucleus rather than a classification based on atomic weight. But the classification derived from the atomic theory *corresponds to* Mendeleef's classification, which was essentially based on empirical generalisations. The modern classification removes the anomalies of the Mendeleef table, and it also provides a position for hydrogen. We can say that the modern atomic theory and electronic theory of valency explain the Mendeleef classification, and the generalisations on which that classification was built.

The modern atomic theory explains the Mendeleef classification not only because it is a source of generalisations which correspond to it, not only because it corrects the table and removes anomalies, but because it enables us to understand *why* the arrangement is so success-ful. Eventually we hope that the present atomic theory will itself come to be explained, and be incorporated into a yet broader scheme. It is in this way that science progresses: theories explain by helping us to comprehend a reality behind appearances and linking it to what we can observe. Each explanatory theory gives deeper insight and, at the same time, organises our knowledge into a larger and more coherent whole. (See pp. 139–40 for Questions and Further Reading related to this chapter.)

6

The Refutation of Laws and Theories

(i) The Refutation of Empirical Generalisations and Laws

In the previous chapter a scientific *law* was defined as an empirical generalisation which was explained by a scientific theory; it was thereby distinguished from a simple empirical generalisation. Examples of simple empirical generalisations are 'All crows are black', 'All dogs bark', 'All men are mortal'. Examples of scientific laws are 'All samples of chlorine gas are green', 'All heavy objects fall to the ground with an acceleration of 32 ft/sec./sec.', 'The pressure of a gas is inversely proportional to its volume at constant temperature'. Because laws are supported by and give support to theories, the refutation of a law is a much more important matter than the refutation of a simple empirical generalisation.

All the same many empirical generalisations, like those listed above, are supported by very extensive experience and we have very considerable confidence in their truth. We should be very surprised to see a red crow, even more surprised to hear a dog moo like a cow, and yet more surprised to meet a man authoritatively known to have lived for 1000 years, who showed no signs of ageing. But the exceptions would not be so fundamentally disturbing as would exceptions to well-established scientific laws. Indeed, in a sense, the exceptions can be seen as being in accordance with wider experience. We have come to accept that there are freaks of nature – we know of many species where colour varies, and we surmise, though less surely, that there could be variations from the characteristic noise made by an animal. What would be surprising would be that the particular oddity of the red crow or the mooing dog had not been observed before — but it would not be incompatible with experience to accept that a certain freak was unique. The case of an apparently immortal man would be less easy to accept, for, in our experience, it would seem that all living things, plants and animals as well as man, eventually perish. Yet there are some kinds of tree that have lived for about 2000 years and could be immortal. We have no *reason* (analogous to the theoretical support for a scientific law) which tells us that another living creature cannot exist for at least as long as those trees and perhaps indefinitely long. Hence, though the existence of a man who had survived for 1000 years and who showed no sign of ageing would astound us, and indeed we should at once suspect fraud, we could come to accept his existence without undermining any corpus of scientific knowledge. This is true of exceptions to any simple empirical generalisation, however extraordinary they may be, and however well confirmed was the generalisation, prior to the exception.

But the case is quite different when we are considering exceptions to scientific laws. An apparent exception to a law not only refutes the relevant empirical generalisation, it will, if accepted, refute or at least lead to some modification of the theory from which the corresponding generalisation can be derived. We are of course considering observations which not only do not support the law, but also do not support generalisations deduced from the propositions of the theory. As was explained in the previous chapter, chapter 5, section iv, it can happen that an empirical law does not give an account so closely in accordance with observation as does the corresponding generalisation deduced from the theory. In such cases the fact that theory 'corrects' the law gives added support to both law and theory. Observations which are in accordance with deduced generalisations, though they technically refute the empirical law, present no problem.

But there can be observations which are not of this sort; they are not in accordance with the law, neither can they be regarded as being in accordance with generalisations deduced from the theory. Say that a purple chlorine gas were prepared, that is, a gas with properties *identical* to that of chlorine save that it was purple, not green. This would be an outright refutation of the law 'All samples of chlorine gas are green'. This generalisation is a law because it can be deduced from the electronic theory of valency, that a gas with the atomic spectrum of chlorine will have a green colour. The imaginary purple gas is to be *exactly* like chlorine, save that it is purple and not green; therefore it would have the spectrum which our theory tells us can only be associated with the green colour. If there is no mistake in observation, the electronic theory of valency must at least be modified, if not rejected. It follows that corresponding generalisations about the colours of other elements will also be in doubt, for they all depend on the same theory. Moreover, the propositions relating spectra and colour are intimately related to propositions concerning energy levels and energy changes which affect the chemical reactivity of elements. The undermining of part of the electronic theory of valency will have repercussions not only on the rest of that theory but also on other associated theories, which would entail very substantial modification of many theories previously regarded as firmly established.

It is as well to point out here that it would be no solution to make the proposition 'All samples of chlorine gas are green' analytically true and so refuse to consider that the purple gas was chlorine. We shall return to this point later, because there are occasions when generalisations do come to be regarded as definitions and therefore analytic truths. But this will not solve the problem here. It is part of the data that the purple gas has all properties like chlorine save that it is purple and not green. Our problem arises because spectral lines thought to be associated with green and only green colour have been found associated with purple colour. Suffice it to say that were such a substance to be reported as observed, and there was no question of trickery, then chemists would insist that there must be some mistake in the techniques of the experiments: either the purple colour, or the recorded spectrum, or both, were the result of some error. Such an artificial example puts the problem much more crudely than is the case when it arises in science as practised. But because it is crude the choice is made clear: either chemists would have to suppose some extraordinary combination of circumstances that led to a mistake which could not be detected, or the fundamental theories of chemistry, and some of physics, would have to be revised.

If no more samples of the purple gas could be prepared, there would be no doubt that the general body of scientists would ascribe the observation to error, however eminent and skilful was the scientist, or group of scientists, who reported it. However, though 'pushed to one side' as an artefact, it would be disturbing, and it could be that an investigator would seek and locate the factors which had made the gas purple rather than green.

But if the purple gas was repeatedly prepared, many workers would be seeking long and hard in the hope of finding the factor in the technique of production which was producing so extraordinary a substance. The search would be for the positive analogy in the methods of preparation of the purple gas which distinguished it from the preparation of the 'normal' green gas. There would also be a search for the positive analogy between the experiments conducted on the measurement of the positions of the spectral lines; the search would be for some factor which would explain why a different colour, that is, purple, was *not* producing a different spectrum. The decisive refutation of the theory, that is, an explanation which involved accepting that the electronic theory was, in this respect at least, just plain wrong, would be avoided. Unless other extraordinary spectra were reported, the case of a purple chlorine, with the spectrum of green chlorine, would be held to be an anomaly, indeed a fantastic paradox, but it would not be allowed to destroy the theory. The theory would be undermined, but not refuted. As we shall see, it is not an easy matter to refute an established theory. (See this chapter, section iv.)

The case of an imaginary purple chlorine is interesting because it is an example of an exception to what may be taken as a 'chemical rule', namely 'All samples of a given element are identical'. Now there are many well-known exceptions to this rule. Some elements show allotropy and can be found in two or more different forms: there is a red and a yellow phosphorus, and there are two forms of oxygen: oxygen and ozone. There are also isotopes of many elements. But the different varieties of an element have always been accounted for, in that they have been shown to be due to variations in molecular or in atomic structure. However, the rule is still a useful guide, and at first might lead the scientist to deny that a purple gas could be chlorine. But it would not be particularly disturbing if he had to admit a new form, or allotrope, of chlorine. The new form would have a different spectrum from the green chlorine. Indeed from the different spectrum the scientist could probably surmise the molecular arrangement which was responsible for the different colour.

(ii) Definitions and Analytic Propositions

A quality of all empirical generalisations is that they can sometimes be used as definitions rather than as descriptions. A definition is a statement as to the meaning or connotation of a word, and, if it is accepted, it becomes an analytic proposition. For example, if 'All samples of a given element are identical' was taken as an analytic proposition, then, by definition, red and yellow phosphorus would be two different elements and so would green and a hypothetical purple chlorine. It so happens that we do not care to take the proposition as a definition, we treat it rather as a guiding rule which has exceptions. But, if in experience there had never been an exception found, then we might take the proposition to be analytic and a proposition that helped to define the word 'element'.

It is salutary to consider the process by which a synthetic proposition, that is, a description potentially refutable by experience, may come to be considered as an analytic proposition if *in fact* it is *not* refuted by experience. It is necessary to study some propositions very carefully, asking ourselves what we should do if there was an exception observed, to decide whether they are being treated as synthetic propositions describing the world, or as analytic propositions telling us the meaning of words. If they are analytic propositions they cannot be refuted by experience; if they are synthetic propositions, that is, true empirical generalisations, then just one well-attested observation, not in accord with the generalisation, will refute it.

Generalisations about the world are arrived at by induction. As was stated in chapter I, it is our early spontaneous inductions which help us to arrive at simple concepts, that is, they enable us to recognize the things around us. We recognise objects such as tables and chairs, apples or people, because we have, by induction, learned that certain properties are associated. Thus a young child living in Exeter might believe that one of the properties regularly associated with a town was a large cathedral in a cathedral close.

A baby regards all the properties which he regularly finds associated as defining properties. For the child, propositions such as 'All crows are black', 'All cats mew', 'All cakes are sweet' are statements of fact in his experience, and he would believe that the generalisations were universally true. Of course this is not to say that a young child consciously regards the propositions as definitions, let alone as being analytically true, but he regards classifying schemes as being much more rigid than in fact they are. In other words, a crow would not be a 'proper' crow if it were not black, a cat would not be quite a cat if it did not mew, a cake would certainly not be regarded as cake if it tasted of roast chicken. The appeal of magic to the child comes when he begins to appreciate that certain properties regularly associated in his experience might not be so associated. He is delighted with the corollary, with the strangeness and novelty of the idea of associating properties which are *not* found associated in his experience: the talking cat, the scarlet crow, the cake that tastes like roast chicken. He comes to appreciate that certain properties can be replaced without necessarily producing an entirely new thing, but rather a familiar thing with strange characteristics. But the child does not seriously consider whether the scarlet crow is still a *kind of* crow, whether the talking cat is still a *kind of* cat, or whether the cake tasting of roast chicken should still be regarded as a *kind of* cake. On a common-sense level we are like the child in that we make statements about the association of properties without reflecting whether the association is or is not a defining feature of the concept. If the question arises, we make an intuitive decision as to whether we are making an analytic statement which defines the word and indicates its connotation, or whether we are making a synthetic statement and learning a fact about some object.

We may intuitively decide that a crow can be a crow without necessarily being black, and that a cat can be a cat without necessarily mewing. It follows then that the generalisations 'All crows are black' and 'All cats mew' will be synthetic statements describing the crows and the cats that have been observed. We would be prepared to grant that if there were a bird in every way like a crow save that it were scarlet, then it would have to be called a crow; likewise a non-mewing cat would still be called a cat. But if we took the opposite view, and the generalisations were regarded as analytic propositions then the scarlet bird would not be called a crow, because to be called a crow a bird *must* be black; for a similar reason the non-mewing animal could not be called a cat. But in actual fact the truth of the matter is that in ordinary language we simply do not think carefully about the significance of our statements; we are not really clear as to which properties of crows or cats are defining properties and which are accidental properties. When we make an empirical generalisation and find that, in experience, there are no exceptions, the decision as to whether our generalisation is a synthetic or analytic proposition does not have to be taken. Life and speech would become very complicated if it were necessary for us to be sure of the connotations of all the words we used and to be quite clear when we were describing and when we were defining.

The same indeterminacy is apparent in many scientific generalisations. Take the generalisations 'Copper melts at 1083°C.' and 'Silver has a specific gravity of 10.47'. Are these propositions contributing to the definition of what we mean by 'copper' and 'silver'? In this case they are analytic propositions and *must* be true. Then a metal, like copper in other respects, but without this melting point would not *be* copper; a metal like silver in other respects but without the particular specific gravity, would not *be* silver. Or are the generalisations synthetic propositions, telling us something about the metals copper and silver but potentially refutable by experience? There is no doubt that the generalisations were *arrived at* by induction from experience. Both for the individual and for mankind the earliest notions of the two metals were based on their appearance. Gradually it came to be appreciated that there were other characteristic qualities associated with each different-looking material, and that these were perhaps easier to measure and more consistently the same. The *appearance* of silver and copper alters as the light falling on them alters; it also alters in that a tarnish film may cover them. But, in our experience, melting point and density (at constant temperature) have remained constant. The difficulty of deciding in such cases whether the relevant generalisations are analytic or synthetic propositions arises from the fact that we do not envisage the possibility of the propositions being untrue, and so it does not matter whether they are held to be analytic or synthetic because this makes absolutely no practical difference. It is not until we are confronted with a situation where a generalisation *fails* to hold that we have to consider whether it is to be taken as an analytic or synthetic proposition.

If we are dealing with simple empirical generalisations, then it is best to be content to let the position remain indeterminate, as we do in everyday speech. Propositions such as 'Copper melts at 1083°C' have an indeterminate status. Scientists would be baffled if a metal like copper with a melting point of 1084°C were produced, and until it is produced it is senseless to debate what view would be taken. But if we are dealing with empirical generalisations which are also scientific laws, that is generalisations like 'All samples of chlorine gas are green', which are supported by a scientific theory, then they are normally treated as synthetic propositions. (Indeed as we saw in the previous section, we do not avoid the problem posed by an exception by taking the proposition as an analytic truth.) A law *must* be a synthetic proposition since it purports to give us knowledge of the empirical world. If it were held to be an analytic proposition it would only be defining a scientific term, and definitions are not empirical laws.

Definitions are used in science of course – scientific terms must be defined. But we must take care when we are using a scientific term in a generalisation, for we may be using a definition or a description. It may be a matter of convenience whether we adopt a generalisation as a definition or whether we leave it as an empirical description. Take the proposition 'All mammals suckle their young'. This is a definition of the word 'mammal', it is therefore an analytic proposition. Having accepted the definition, we may make empirical generalisations about mammals. We find from experience that a large number of different sorts of mammal produce their young viviparously and that they are land animals. By induction we arrive at two more generalisations: 'Mammals produce their young viviparously' and 'Mammals are land animals'. Then it is observed that whales and dolphins suckle their young. Are they to be classed as mammals even though they are sea animals? The answer is 'Yes', because the generalisation 'Mammals are land animals' was *not* a definition of the word 'mammal', it was a description of mammals. It was a synthetic proposition which has been found to be false. The generalisation 'Mammals produce their young viviparously' is also false because the duck-billed platypus suckles its young (and is therefore a mammal), but it lays eggs.

The two generalisations 'Mammals are land animals' and 'Mammals produce their young viviparously' were genuine empirical generalisations based on experience and were therefore refutable by experience. But the question as to whether they were synthetic or analytic might not have been considered if exceptions had not been observed. However, since exceptions *were* observed it was decided that it was more convenient to *define* the class of mammals, such that the word 'mammal' only entailed that mammals suckled their young; this was the definition. Definitions are arbitrary, but they are not unscientific; quite the contrary – they are essential to science. Until we do have a scheme of classification and words with fixed connotations we cannot progress. Clear definition of words is necessary if we are to agree on what concepts we possess. We must be able to say *why* a given animal is said to be a mammal, and how the word 'mammal' is used.

It must be clear that the decision to define a word, and therefore a class of phenomena, in a certain way is not *entirely* arbitrary. We have seen that it is not clear what *are* the *defining* properties of copper or silver. There are several properties which are used to define copper:

melting point, density, atomic structure etc. The precision of the definition is a consequence of our unrefuted experience of these properties being regularly associated. The descriptive term 'mammal' *seems* more artificial than 'copper'. It represents a group of many different kinds of animals, a group of animals which are distinguished from others because they suckle their young. Greater sophistication was needed to regard this group as distinct enough to need a special word, because variations within the group (for example, between elephants and guinea pigs) seems so much greater than the similarity which classes them together. By contrast, the group of materials called 'copper', and even the group of materials called 'metals' are much more alike. But the principle by which mammals were adopted as a distinct group, the principle of the classification, arose from experience: it was convenient to classify animals that suckled their young into one special group because experience revealed that such animals were more advanced biologically. Further experience might have shown that this classification was not helpful – just as further experience did show that the classification of elements as metals and non-metals was not helpful. Thus, though the decision of how the class is defined is arbitrary, it is not divorced from experience because the classifications that are made are ones which experience reveals as being helpful. The definitions are analytically true statements, but of course we can decide to discard them if experience has shown that they are of no great use.

To summarise, we may say that all empirical generalisations are based on experience. If they are supported by a theory, and so are scientific laws, they must be synthetic statements and potentially refutable by experience. There are also many simple empirical generalisations which are synthetic statements, for instance 'All swans are white', 'All crows are black', and these too stand to be refuted by experience. But there are some simple empirical generalisations of indeterminate status, such as 'Copper melts at 1083°C'; they are of indeterminate status because they have not been refuted by experience, and it is not expected that they will be refuted or even could be refuted. Lastly there are analytically true statements which have the form of empirical generalisations. These are definitions, such as 'All mammals suckle their young'. Definitions are arbitrary and their truth is not dependent on experience directly, but if experience shows they are not helpful, the definition may be discarded.

(iii) The Logical Relations of Theories, Laws and Observation Statements

Before considering the process of refutation of scientific theories via the refutation of scientific laws, it is necessary to study the logical relations between observation statements, laws and theories. It is helpful to regard them as propositions which can be related, at least in part, as though they were propositions in a deductive system.

In deductive logic, if we have a proposition p from which various other propositions can be logically deduced: q_0, q_1, q_2 etc., the relation can be formulated as one of strict implication or entailment. The proposition p is called the antecedent, the propositions q_0, q_1, q_2, etc. are called the consequents. The relations can be expressed as:

$$\text{If } p \text{ then } q_0$$
$$\text{If } p \text{ then } q_1$$
$$\text{If } p \text{ then } q_2 \text{ etc.}$$

In logic we are concerned with propositions which can be said to be either *true* or *false*. In the case of a simple empirical proposition the truth value (that is, whether the proposition *is* true or false) of the proposition must be established by observation – direct or indirect. In the case of a compound proposition, composed of two or more simple propositions, the truth value is determined by the truth value of the simple propositions from which it is formed and by the way these are connected.

Where any two propositions are combined by 'if' before the antecedent and 'then' before the consequent, we have an implication of some sort. But it need not be strict implication, and since some other types of implication are involved in science, we should briefly consider certain different types of implicative propositions.

(1) If the attraction between two masses is inversely proportional to the square of the distance between them, and there is a sun with one ambient planet, then the orbits of the planet will be an ellipse with the sun in one focus.

(2) If an animal has more than six legs then it is not an insect.

(3) If a piece of litmus is placed in acid then it will turn pink

(4) If the phlogiston theory is true then I can fly out of the window.

The first relation is an example of strict implication: the consequent can be logically (and this includes mathematical calculations) deduced from the antecedent. In this case the antecedent is a proposition pertaining to a scientific theory plus an assertion of existence, and the consequent is a scientific law. This was how Kepler stated his law for *all* the planets, but this law must be qualified (see chapter 3, section i and chapter 6, section iv).

The second relation also involves strict implication but antecedent follows consequent as the result of the definition of an insect, which must have six legs. It can therefore be said to be implication by definition.

The third relation is an example of causal implication. The consequent does not follow logically from the antecedent, but we know as a matter of fact that they are connected. The fact is established by observation. Empirical generalisations can be put in this form and so can scientific laws. For instance we could say: 'If Mars is a planet then it will have an elliptical orbit round the sun.' As stated in chapter 5, section ii, the scientific laws (as opposed to empirical generalisations) may also be deduced from a scientific theory. Nevertheless it can be expressed (as shown above) as a causal implication.

The fourth relation is an example of material implication. This is the weakest type of implication since the consequent does not follow the antecedent in virtue of logic, definition or causal connection. There need be no kind of rational connection between antecedent and consequent.

Yet all of these implications are of the form: 'If p then q'. What do they have in common? What they have in common is the same truth value dependence; if the implication of whatever kind is to be true, then it can never be the case that p is true when q is false. But for all other truth values of p and q the implication is true. Thus if p is false, q can be true or false, and if q is true p can be true or false.

Implications (1), (2) and (3) have other restrictions: for type (1) there must be the possibility of logical deduction, for type (2) there must be an accepted definition, for type (3) there must be an established causal connection. But, as far as material implication goes, the only restriction on its truth value is that if p is true, then q must be true in order for the implication to be accepted as true. Material implications are commonly used to deny the truth of the antecedent in a picturesque way. As explained above, if the antecedent is false then the whole implication is taken to be true; so we state our false antecedent and then link it to a patently absurd consequent. This emphasises the falsity of the antecedent, for that antecedent *must* be false if the whole implication is accepted as true.

It is important to note that if a consequent is established as true, the antecedent can be true or false, and the whole implication will hold as true. However many consequents of a given antecedent have been established as true, we cannot deduce that the antecedent itself is true. Thus, if from an antecedent p, we have consequents q_0, q_1, q_2 etc. and we know that q_0, q_1, q_2, etc. are true, it need not necessarily be the case that p is true. On the other hand, if we establish that a consequent is false, the antecedent must also be false if the whole implication is to be accepted as true.

In our examples, if we establish that the orbits of the planets are ellipses (and the other laws of Kepler and Galileo that can be deduced from the theory) this does not *prove* that the theory is true. But if only *one* of those laws can be shown to be false then the theory is undermined. (But see also next section.)

From the remarks made about Popper's presentation of the hypothetico-deductive system (chapter 4 section vii), we can see how he uses this logical pattern. Let us call the set of propositions pertaining to a theory as T propositions, law propositions L, and propositions describing what is observed as O propositions. Then if the set T is true, any deducible law L will be true, and if a law L is true then any observation proposition logically deduced from it will be true. To take another example, if propositions of the kinetic theory of gases are true, then Boyle's law and Charles's law will be true. If these L propositions are true we can deduce an indefinitely large number of O propositions about the volume of gases at specified temperatures and pressures, and these can be tested by direct observation. More generally, if T is true then L_0, L_1, L_2 etc. are true, where L_0, L_1, L_2 etc. are deducible from T. If L_0 is true then O_0, O_1, O_2 etc. are true, where these are propositions deducible from L. If L_1 is true then other observation statements O_0', O_1', O_2' etc. are true where these are propositions deducible from L_1. But, however large a number of O propositions are shown to be true, there is no logical ground for asserting that the corresponding L proposition is true. And, in like manner, however many L propositions are accepted, by being taken as empirically established by O propositions, there is no *logical* ground for taking the relevant T propositions, or theory, to be true. On the other hand, if we find that even one O proposition is false then we can *logically* deduce that the corresponding L proposition is false; and if an L proposition is false the relevant T propositions (the theory) can be regarded as having been shown logically to be false. It is because falsification *seems* (but see next section) to be logically certain, whereas verification cannot be, that Popper regards falsification as not only the best but effectively the only method for testing laws and theories.

One more point should be made about the logical structure involved in implication. If a theory and its T propositions are false, it does not follow that the L propositions deduced from it will be false, and similarly if an L proposition is false it does not follow that the O propositions deduced from it will be false. It is perfectly possible for a true conclusion to be arrived at by valid argument from false premises. A simple example is:

All people who have died in the White House were American Presidents
Abraham Lincoln died in the White House
Therefore Abraham Lincoln was an American President

To take an example from empirical science, we can consider the Ptolemaic theory of the cosmos, with a stationary central earth surrounded by sun, moon and planets moving in complicated paths. This theory was a source of true predictions, that is, observation statements which were regarded as adequate for over 1500 years. Admittedly doubts were arising by the early sixteenth century, but *no* theory will yield observation statements precisely in accordance with what is observed (again see next section). All our empirical propositions – theories, laws and observation statements – must simplify experience to make it coherent and comprehensible. We take these propositions to be true in a relative sense, relative to the accuracy we require; they cannot be regarded as true in an absolute sense. Hence the objection that the Ptolemaic theory was yielding *slightly* inaccurate predictions was not at first regarded as a refutation. The theory was false, we now take it as false, but it was the source of true and therefore valuable predictions for many years.

(iv) The Refutation of Theories

But what if an observation statement is false – that is, direct observation is *not* in accordance with the propositions derived from law or theory? We can deduce logically that if O_0 is false then L_0 and T are false, and that if O_0' is false then L_1 and T are false etc. In other words, if one and only one O statement is false it would seem that the relevant law and theory would be conclusively refuted. This is the argument which Popper uses in his account of the testing and corroboration of theories. No observations can conclusively establish the truth of a law or theory, but they can refute it. Scientific tests are designed, says Popper, with the idea of attempting to falsify a law or theory. A good empirical law or theory is one which, so to speak, 'stretches out its neck' and has concrete and specific observational consequences that make it relatively easy to attempt to falsify it. One of the reasons that a scientific law or even a simple empirical generalisation, precisely expressed, is better than the corresponding common-sense generalisation is that the latter is usually expressed so vaguely that it is much less easy to refute.

However, refutation is not so simple as logical considerations might lead us to suppose. It has already been stated that a theory may have consequences which are in closer accordance with observation than those derived from the related law. The theory 'corrects' the law. But, though logically the law is refuted, the theory may also indicate those conditions under which the law would hold, and, if these conditions are unattainable in practice, the theory will yet indicate the conditions under which the law would approach accordance with observation. Empirical descriptions are much more complicated than logical propositions and every empirical law or theory in fact presupposes other propositions about conditions which, though unstated, must be true if the law is to hold and the theory is to be true.

However, if the law and theory are to be *scientific*, it must be possible to state the propositions describing the implied conditions *if this is required*. In the case of Boyle's law we state that the temperature must be constant. More accurate observation shows us that, even holding temperature constant, the law is not strictly true. Now we cannot simply say vaguely that there must be some other factors, we must be specific. Our theory shows us that the conditions under which the law will at least approach the truth, that is, will be in accordance with accurate observation, are those of low pressure and high temperature. We take the law to be corrected by the theory. But we have to admit that, even allowing for corrections by the theory, the law is still not quite in accordance with observation. We cannot simply say that there are unspecified factors which would account for the discrepancy. The discrepancy between consequences predicted by law 'corrected' by theory and observation reflects the complexity of our experience and of the empirical world. No generalisation, however much qualified by theory, will be quite in accordance with observation.

Thus in one sense any observation may be said to *refute* a law or theory, though, in practice, we accept that observation supports law and/or theory if there is accordance within certain specified limits. Moreover, having accepted this, there is a sense in which observation can always be made to *support* a law and/or theory. If there is a discrepancy we will always look for an explanation which does not involve refuting the law and/or theory. Here we must leave the strictly logical relation between observation, law and theory, for we assume that there is some factor which would account for the apparent conflict between observation and law or theory.

If a well-established law, such as Boyle's law, appeared to be refuted by a well-attested observation, that is, refuted in the sense that the discrepancy between what was observed and what was predicted could not be accounted for by the kinetic theory of gases, then both law and theory would be undermined. But before the refutation was accepted there would be many factors to check, and many things which would be doubted before the law and theory were seriously jeopardised. First there would be a check for some undetected factor, such as a change in temperature which had been overlooked, or a leak in the apparatus. Then the reliability of the instruments used would be questioned: the pressure gauge, the thermometer, even the shape of the gas container. Then there would be the possibility that some *other* law, which was the basis for calculating pressure or volume, was false. When we test a given law such as Boyle's law, we will almost certainly have to assume that some other law is true, for example, the law of expansion of mercury with rise in temperature. For the purpose of testing Boyle's law, the heat expansion law would be assumed to be true – it would be used as a *functionally analytic* statement. To assume that a given law is true presents no problem *if* the law which is being tested is confirmed. But if observation appears to refute that law, then it may be *because* some other law, which had been assumed to be indubitable, that is, functionally analytic, is in fact false. It might for instance be considered that if Boyle's law appeared to be refuted by observation, then it was more likely that the law relating to the expansion of mercury (which had been taken as functionally analytic) was in fact false. It would then become necessary to test *this* law by another experiment of a different type.

Thus if observation appears to refute an established law and therefore an established theory, refutation does not follow as a logical consequence, even if the observation is well attested. Firstly there will be a search for error in the type of experiment, then instruments will be checked, and finally other laws, taken previously as being functionally analytic, will be called into question and perhaps tested. It is only if all these appear to be free of error that the established law and theory will be undermined. But it is to be emphasised that though the process of refutation is not a simple matter, yet, at the last, both law and theory must be held to be synthetic statements; they must be put to the test of experiment and they must be shown to be in accordance with observation. If all efforts to save the law and theory are unsuccessful, then they must at least be modified if not rejected.

But very often refuting, or apparently refuting, observations *are* found to be due to error or to some hitherto unknown and/or undetected factor. For example, in the early nineteenth century it was observed that the planet Uranus did not follow the path predicted by Newton's theory. Observations appeared to refute the theory, and repeated observations confirmed the discrepancy. One possibility was that Newton's theory did not apply to masses in regions remote from the earth, but this explanation was not regarded with favour. Another possibility was that there was some disturbing factor, such as a remote planet. Calculations showed that part of the heavens where such a disturbing planet might be found, and it was thus that the planet called Neptune was discovered. It is to be noted that the probability of there being a planet in that particular part of the heavens was small if Newton's theory were not true. The fact that the planet was found was therefore very strong corroboration of the theory. In this case an apparent refutation came to bring even greater support for the theory. But predictions made by Einstein, in the early twentieth century, on the basis of his special theory of relativity, did at last lead to the refutation, or rather modification, of Newton's theory. Here we have an example of a well-established empirical theory being corrected and replaced by a more general theory. The ultimate test, and the decision to replace a theory, depends and must depend on the evidence supplied by observation. It would always be possible to 'save' Newton's theory by an appeal to some undetected factor, an appeal to inaccuracy of measurement or even by casting doubt on some other theory. But, as in this case, if at the last none of the appeals are successful then the theory must go.

To summarise, we may say that the relation of theories and laws to each other and to observation statements may be compared to that of strict implication in deductive logic. We may see that just as in strict implication if the antecedent p is true, the consequent q must be true, so, likewise, if the theory is true the derived law must be true, and if theory or law is true then the relevant observation statements must be true. But the converse does not hold. In logic to assert that if the consequent is true then the antecedent must be true is called the fallacy of affirming the consequent. However many consequents are true, it is not possible to deduce logically that the antecedent is true. Likewise, however many observation statements are true it is not possible to deduce that the corresponding law or theory is true. In addition, however many laws are accepted as true it is not possible to deduce that the corresponding theory is true. But in logic we can at least deduce a *false* antecedent from a false consequent. This cannot be done so simply in empirical science. An observation statement not supported by observation undermines the corresponding law and theory, but many other observations may need to be made before either law or theory is regarded as decisively refuted.

There is more to empirical science than logical relations. Well-confirmed observations can and do bring us to regard many laws and theories as true. But we must never become dogmatic – the best attested law and theories may well be modified. On the other hand we cannot take a well-attested observation as being logically certain to refute a law and therefore a theory. Experience is complex, and the process of refutation may need many carefully controlled experiments. It is always possible to 'save' a given law and/or theory at the expense of some other law and/or theory. Yet empirical science cannot be far removed from observation and it is, at the last, observation which will decide. We cannot save a law or theory indefinitely by maintaining that there must be some undetected factor which would account for the lack of accordance between observation statement and observation. This would be to make empirical laws, and therefore empirical theories, irrefutable by experience, and this is directly contrary to the spirit of scientific enquiry. Such laws and theories would cease to be *scientific* laws and theories, they would become either analytic definitions or metaphysical theories, and they would not relate directly to the world of experience. (See pp. 140–1 for Questions and Further Reading related to this chapter.)

7

The Relation of Cause and Effect

(i) Animistic Notions of Cause

If A causes B, then A is followed by B. This might be an everyday account of the meaning of *cause*. Yet it might be objected that in everyday, common-sense thought the notion of *cause* conveys more than a sequence of events; there is a hint of some underlying relationship between cause and effect which is responsible for the observed sequence. The underlying relationship *necessitates* that B, the effect, follows A, the cause. A study of cause and effect must take account of this, even if only to show that the notion of necessary causal relation is purely psychological, being grounded merely on the experience of invariable sequence. Let us consider some examples of cause and effect to help throw some light on the relation of cause and effect.

We say that a push *causes* a ball to roll along the ground, and that to tread on someone's toe is to *cause* them to feel pain. Both of the instances cited are examples of causes which are due to the action of some thinking agent – though the agent may not have been thinking of producing the effect at the time of his action, for he may accidentally have pushed the ball or have trodden on the toe. Nevertheless, since the actions could have been taken with the effect in view, it is no great step to regard the agent as *willing* the effect, and achieving the effect, via the cause. Because so many effects are achieved by ourselves and others performing one action which it is expected will be followed by the desired effect, there is a *tendency*, quite marked amongst the relatively uneducated, but not unnoticeable amongst others, to regard causes as in some sense dependent upon agents, and even of conscious agents, who are *willing* the effect. This animistic attitude to cause is the result of primitive belief – the belief that all nature, rocks and rivers, as well as men and animals, is imbued with a conscious spirit.

The attitude is present in Aristotle's account of causes. He described four types of cause which might all be considered as causes of a given effect. There were materials in which the change took place, these were the material cause(s); there was the plan to be followed, this was the formal cause; there was an agent or source of movement to alter the materials, this was the efficient cause; and there was the purpose of the change, this was the final cause. An analysis like that of Aristotle's is very appropriate if we consider such changes as the making of a vase or the building of a ship, that is, if we consider changes brought about by a conscious agent, where there is a definite end, the effect, in view. But the tendency to regard all changes as being due to the action of a conscious agent must be resisted; there are plenty of cause-and-effect relations where the notion of the cause being the action of a conscious agent can only be a relic of primitive animism. Thus the rise of the river Arno caused the destruction of many valuable manuscripts in Florence, but we should not say that the cause of the damage was the anger of the river god.

If we are to study the question of *causal essence* and whether there is some intrinsic relation between cause and effect, we must begin by rejecting all animistic views of cause. This does not mean that we must completely reject the notion of an agent. It may be helpful to think of a cause as a 'thing', as long as we do not think of it as a *conscious* agent willing some effect. For example, a spark may be said to cause an explosion, a stone may be said to cause the breaking of a window or rain may be said to cause the wetness of a road.

However, if we consider carefully, there can be no reason why we should not regard a cause as a thing *or* as an event, for there is no absolute distinction between 'things' and 'events'. We can say that a thing acts as a cause; or we can say that an event, that is, the involvement of a thing in a process, acts as a cause. Thus the spark considered as a thing can be the cause of an explosion, or the spark as a provider of heat can be considered as an event causing the process of the explosion. Similarly we can say that the stone broke the window, or the stone in the process of moving broke the window. Things can themselves be regarded as processes and therefore as events. It is relatively easy to see how a spark can be regarded as a process – it is part of a process of combustion. In the same way we can regard the thing we call the sun as a process. But it is less easy to regard such relatively stable things as stones or water as processes. Yet they can be seen as processes: the stone can be seen as a moving thing, the water can be seen falling as rain; these are processes.

Analogously, we can consider events as things. An explosion can be regarded as a thing rather than as an event. The breaking of a window can be regarded as a phenomenon. It is partly a matter of habit, and partly a matter of the situation, whether we decide to regard a phenomenon as a thing or as an event or process. Hence we may regard certain causes as things and other causes as processes or events. Indeed we may choose to view some causes from both aspects.

Whether causes are regarded as things, or as processes (events), or whether they are viewed as both things and events, we can agree that they do not represent a conscious agent. Yet allowing no conscious agent, we are dissatisfied with the relation between cause and effect being described solely as a sequence of events or phenomena. Day invariably follows night, but we do not regard night as *causing* day; there is something more to causal relations than mere sequence.

(ii) Necessary and Sufficient Conditions

To arrive at what underlies the notion of cause, we must first distinguish two aspects of causes: necessary conditions and sufficient conditions. In any actual situation no single event or thing can be isolated as the *sole* cause; there are many relevant factors each contributing to the effect. When it is said that some one factor *caused* the effect, what is meant is that, *given all the relevant conditions,* this one factor was a sufficient condition to produce the effect. But there were many other conditions which were necessary. Now, though we cannot always know, let alone specify, *all* the relevant conditions it does not follow that it becomes pointless to assert that a given factor was the cause of an effect. It is taken for granted when we assert that a given event or thing is a sufficient condition for an effect, that the various background but necessary conditions are satisfied. This can be so even if we are unable to specify exactly what these conditions would be. The examples given so far:

The push causing the ball to move
The tread on the toe causing pain
Rain causing wet streets
The stone causing the breaking of the window
A spark causing an explosion

are examples of sufficient conditions, that is, given the condition, the effect follows.

When the word 'cause' is used without any qualification it is generally 'sufficient condition' which is intended. A moment's thought will show that though the causes listed above are regarded as conditions sufficient to produce the effect, they are only sufficient if a great many other conditions are satisfied. The ball must be on a smooth horizontal surface to roll, it must not be so large that the push is too small to disturb it etc. The toe must not be protected by a tough shoe if there is to be pain, the tread must be heavy enough etc. The pavements must not be protected by a tarpaulin if the rain is to wet them. The stone must be thrown hard enough to break the window. The gases must be present in certain proportions if there is to be an explosion. When we speak of a cause being sufficient to produce the effect we assume that many other factors and circumstances which would generally be expected to operate and occur, *do* in fact operate and occur. These other factors are called the *necessary conditions*, for without their presence the effect could not occur. But they alone may not be sufficient for the effect to occur. A sufficient condition is sufficient to produce the effect, *assuming that* all the necessary conditions are operating; generally this means assuming normal or 'expected' circumstances.

Given that a cause is a sufficient condition, it follows that the effect is necessary to the cause, that is, the effect invariably follows the cause. We have 'If C_s then E'. If the condition C_s is present then the effect must follow; that is, since the cause is sufficient for the effect, the effect necessarily follows the cause. We can also say that if the effect is not observed there cannot have been the sufficient condition. This may be expressed as 'No E then no C_s '.

Let us look at the examples: a push is sufficient to roll the ball; if there is a push the ball must roll, and moreover, if the ball does not roll there can have been no push. A tread on the toe is sufficient to cause pain; if there is a tread on the toe there will be pain, and moreover, if there is no pain there can have been no tread on the toe. Rain is sufficient to wet the pavement; if there is rain the pavements must become wet, and moreover, if the pavements are not wet there cannot have been rain. The thrown stone is sufficient to break the window; if the stone is thrown the window must break, and moreover, if the window does not break the stone cannot have been thrown. A spark is sufficient to cause an explosion; if there is a spark there must be an explosion, and moreover, if there is no explosion there can have been no spark.

But none of the above sufficient conditions are *necessary* to the production of the effect. In the above examples it would be possible to have the effects without the particular sufficient conditions. The ball could roll for some reason other than a push; pain might be caused by other means than treading on the toe; the streets might be wet though it was not raining etc.

It is thus that a sufficient condition is to be contrasted with a necessary condition, that is, a condition which must operate if the effect is to follow. In the case of necessary conditions, if the condition does not operate then there is no effect, and therefore if we *do* have the effect then we know that the necessary condition must have operated. The relation between necessary condition and effect is the converse of the relation between sufficient condition and effect.

With necessary condition we have:
  The condition C_n is necessary for the effect E, i.e., C_n must obtain if there is E
  No condition C_n, then no effect E
  If there is effect E, then there must be condition
  The effect E is sufficient for the condition

With sufficient condition we have:
  The condition C_s is sufficient for the effect E
  If there is the condition C_s then there must be the effect E (i.e., E invariably follows)
  No effect E, then no condition C_s
  The effect E is necessary for the condition C_s, i.e., E necessarily accompanies C_s

A necessary condition *must* be present for an effect, but it alone is not sufficient to bring about the effect. This is why, when we speak of 'cause', unqualified, usually we are taken to mean 'sufficient condition'; for by 'cause' we generally refer to an event or phenomenon which is to be followed by the effect, we do not generally mean an event or phenomenon which is merely necessary for there to be the possibility of the effect. Examples of necessary conditions are the possession of eyes in order to detect bacteria under the microscope, the attainment of a necessary grade in gymnastics before being able to graduate from a military academy, the possession of one positive charge on the nucleus of an atom in order to be the heavy hydrogen isotope, deuterium. In such cases, although the conditions are necessary for the effects, they are not in themselves sufficient. To detect bacteria we must have eyes, but the microscope must be working properly and the specimen must have been exposed at the right temperature etc. To graduate from the military academy it is necessary to have a certain proficiency in gymnastics, but this alone will not be sufficient, proficiency must be shown in other fields. It is necessary to have one, and only one, positive charge on the nucleus to be an atom of deuterium, but this does not suffice to distinguish deuterium from ordinary hydrogen or from the other isotope, tritium.

A cause which is both necessary and sufficient to produce a given effect is one of which we can say that the effect must follow the cause, (showing that the cause is a sufficient condition) and the cause must operate for the effect (showing that it is a necessary condition). Without the cause there will be no effect, and without the effect the cause could not have been. An example of a necessary and sufficient cause is the burning of sodium, which is a necessary and sufficient condition of the characteristic spectrum of sodium, considered as an effect. Another example is the passing of an electric current, via platinum electrodes, through very dilute sulphuric acid solution; this is a necessary and sufficient condition for the production of hydrogen and oxygen from the water of the solution. However, we must bear in mind, when considering such conditions, the qualification made with regard to sufficient conditions, namely that they were *sufficient*, assuming normal or 'expected' background conditions. This applies also to the sufficiency of necessary and sufficient conditions. In the given examples we have assumed, among many other things, that, in the first case, the light from a sodium lamp is passed through the spectrometer in the normal way; in the second case we have assumed that the solution is at ordinary laboratory temperature, and that there are no materials in the solution save sulphuric acid and water.

We now see that our question as to some relation between cause and effect must be rephrased, taking account of whether the cause is a necessary condition, a sufficient condition, or a necessary and sufficient condition. If the cause is a necessary condition are we saying that there is something about the effect which *requires* the cause? If the cause is a sufficient condition are we saying that there is something about the cause which *requires* the effect? If the cause is a necessary and sufficient condition are we saying that cause and effect require each other? Certainly we seem to intend something more than mere sequence.

(iii) The Causal Relation as a Law

Up to this point the relation of cause and effect has been treated as one which involves a temporal sequence of events. The sequence is invariable in that either the effect must follow the cause (sufficient condition) or the cause must precede the effect (necessary condition). It is the common-sense approach: cause and effect have a time order in our thought. This is partly a result of our notion of cause arising from a conscious agent, but it is also because the two events or phenomena may themselves be regarded as the start and finish of a process of change which occurs in a given space of time.

But there is a totally different way of looking at cause and effect which leads us to avoid the notion of temporal sequence, and which at the same time may explain why the relation between cause and effect seems to be something more than that of an invariable sequence. Causes and effects can be regarded as illustrating some empirical generalisation or law. When someone says that A causes B, he is really saying that this is a particular instance of the general law that A-things or A-events are invariably associated with B-things or with B-events. For example:

(1) Rain causes wet pavements
(2) Increase of electromotive force applied to a circuit causes increase in current
(3) Increase in pressure of a gas causes a corresponding decrease in volume, if temperature is constant

All these causal relationships can be reformulated as:

(1) A sign of rain is that pavements are wet
(2) The current in a circuit is proportional to the applied electro-motive force
(3) The pressure of a gas is inversely proportional to its volume (at constant temperature).

The first generalisation asserts a simple association of properties. The most simple causal relations can be reformulated as empirical generalisations of this sort, though it must always be possible to suggest a reason for the association. In this case the reason is obvious: rain is water and will wet everything that it touches. But there are some empirical generalisations which cannot be 'explained'. We can give no explanation of the generalisation 'All crows are black'. Hence we do not reformulate this generalisation as a causal relationship. It sounds odd to assert 'Being a crow causes blackness'.

The second generalisation appears more like a scientific law. This generalisation can be related to other empirical generalisations and is well-enough attested to be reformulated as a causal relationship. The concept of the resistance of an electric circuit is bound up with Ohm's empirical discovery that current was directly proportional to voltage. The unit of resistance, the ohm, is defined in terms of unit current and voltage. It can be shown that the resistance of a conductor can be related to the material of the conductor, its shape, and its temperature. The law known as Ohm's law can be shown to apply to all the very large number of conducting materials: to metals, to non-metals such as carbon, and to solutions. We regard it as possible to reformulate the relationship of current and electromotive force as a causal relationship.

However, this particular relationship, and also the relationship given by Boyle's law, illustrate that what we take to be the *cause* is entirely the result of the way in which we happen to think of the system and of the process occurring in it. In any given process we take one event to be initiating the change, and this prior event is thought of as the *cause*; the other event becomes the effect, but if two factors are related by a numerical law, either one of them can be thought of as a cause. For example, if we imagine the process of changing the batteries or the source of electromotive force for the circuit, we will regard the change of electromotive force as being the cause, and the consequent change in the current as being the effect. But if we imagine a flow of the current through a given length of wire as producing a change in electric potential across the wire, then we regard the flow of the current as being the cause of the change in electric potential, that is, the change in the electric potential is regarded as an effect. So in the case of current and electromotive force; either one can be regarded as the cause or the effect. A corresponding view can be taken of the relationship between pressure and volume which is given by Boyle's law. If we imagine a change of pressure on the gas, then we hold that this will cause a change in volume. But if we imagine the gas as being confined in a larger or smaller space, then we hold that the change in volume will cause a corresponding change in gas pressure.

Causal relations can be reformulated as associations of properties or as numerical relations between values of properties. These may be expressed as laws or as well-established empirical generalisations. Such laws and generalisations allow us to predict the outcome of a process occurring in a given system. The law itself is non-temporal in character whereas the process is temporal. An account of a given process may be made in terms of cause and effect rather than of laws. Cause and effect accounts reinforce the temporal aspect of process. What is considered as a cause and what is considered as an effect depend on what sort of process is described. Sometimes cause and effect may be interchanged according to the mode of presentation or the mode of thought about the process.

Now let us consider the generalisation 'Day follows night'. There is no doubt that this can be regarded as a scientific law, and yet we do not reformulate it as a causal relation, namely 'Night causes day'. The causal relation must not only be a law-like sequence, it must describe the beginning and end of a process. To say 'Night causes day' is to imply that there is a direct connection, such that a process started by night would be ended by day; this is clearly not the case. The process is started by the rotation of the earth round the sun and ends in the observed sequence, one complete rotation giving one sequence. We do have a causal relation, but it is the proposition 'The rotation of the earth as it moves round the sun causes the alternation of night and day'; this can be reformulated as the non-temporal law 'The alternation of night and day is associated with the rotation of the earth round the sun'.

Thus there *is* more to causal relationship than mere sequence of events or of phenomena. To be understood as a causal relationship, it must be possible to reformulate the sequence as a well-attested empirical generalisation and/or as a numerical relation of values of properties, and/or as a scientific law. Moreover the generalisation or law must be one which directly links cause and effect. Both necessary and sufficient causal relations can be reformulated in this way. We say that pressure is inversely related to volume of a gas; we can take either pressure or volume change as starting a process and therefore acting as a sufficient condition. But another feature of the law is that temperature must remain constant, and this factor is a necessary condition for the effect. All the background or 'normal' conditions are necessary conditions, and they are always implied by the law, though they may not be explicitly stated.

(iv) Mill's Canons of Induction

To search for the cause (or causes) of an effect, or for the effect (or effects) of some cause, is to seek a causal relation and therefore to seek an empirical generalisation or law. John Stuart Mill thought that the search could be entirely a matter of experiment and observation. He thought that generalisations from particular observations could be confirmed and so become well-attested. He did not reject the notion of explanatory theory, he appreciated that a law could be derived from a theory, and theory could therefore be a guide to experiment. But he did not appreciate that unless there is always at least some vague hypothesis as to what sort of generalisation might be true, the experimenter cannot begin to appreciate which of the very large number of possible observations are likely to be relevant.

Because it rested on the notion of generalising from particular observations, Mill called his method of experimental enquiry an *inductive* method. Quite apart from his minimising the importance of theory and hypothesis, Mill's account has been criticised on other grounds, and we shall consider some of these criticisms. But it is true to say that Mill's account does describe procedures for testing hypotheses, and for testing suggested causal relationships. His method does not give an account of discovery, as he thought it did, but it does show how discoveries can be supported by experimental investigation and/or by straight observation. Therefore Mill does convey the procedure and principles on which the scientist *as experimenter*, rather than as discoverer, acts.

Mill began by laying down two principles which governed the rules which he was to formulate. The principles were that nothing which was absent when an occurrence happened could be its cause, and that nothing which was present when an occurrence failed to happen could be its cause. In fact these principles should be more carefully formulated as 'Nothing which is absent when an event occurs can be its necessary condition, and nothing which is present when an event fails to occur can be its sufficient condition'. But, as we shall see, Mill did not distinguish necessary and sufficient conditions.

However, the two principles, even as formulated by Mill, are the basis of what may be called *eliminative induction*. If we look for a cause of a given effect we will find a large number of factors which accompany the effect, and it is perfectly true that any of them could be a sufficient and/or necessary cause of the effect. But if we find an instance where a factor is present and the effect does not occur, then we know that at least that factor was not a sufficient cause. If we find one instance where the effect does occur and a certain factor is *not* present, then that factor can be eliminated as a possible necessary cause.

The elimination is certain; it is analogous to the falsifying of a law or theory by observation. As we saw in the previous chapter, section iii, though in practice refutation may be difficult, there will come a point, when all allowances have been made, when the law or theory, *must* be in accordance with observation if it is not to be rejected, or at least modified. Analogously, though the testing of causal relations is complicated by possibilities of multiple and interacting causes and effects, the test of observation is final. We can show that a given hypothesis as to causal relation is *false*. But, just as it is not possible to establish a theory or law as true beyond question, so we cannot establish a given factor as a *certain* necessary and/or sufficient condition. Undoubtedly we cannot establish the certain truth of a causal relation by collecting a large number of instances which confirm it. Generalisations which are based simply on a large number of positive instances are the result of what is called *simple induction*, or *induction by enumeration*. It is notoriously unreliable because no attempt is made to look for an instance which might falsify the relationship. But a hypothesis which resists attempts at falsification is well confirmed. Experimental tests should therefore be designed for the attempt to falsify rather than to find supporting evidence.

As has been remarked, Mill did not distinguish between necessary and sufficient conditions, and because of this he could not distinguish an effect which was sufficient for the cause (if the cause were a necessary condition) from an effect which necessarily followed from the cause (if the cause were a sufficient condition). Also, as was noted, Mill did not appreciate the importance of a hypothesis as to cause: moreover as he expounds his Methods, it is necessary that the instances observed have only one circumstance in common, or differ by only one circumstance. This is clearly impossible. Mill disregarded an essential factor for the success of his Methods, namely that there must be some guiding hypothesis which will indicate what factors or groups of factors are *relevant*. It may be possible to find instances which have only *one relevant* circumstance in common, and to find instances which differ by only *one relevant* circumstance.

The first Method, the Method of Agreement, was stated by Mill as:

> If two or more instances of the phenomenon under investigation have only one circumstance in common, the circumstance in which alone all the instances agree is the cause (or effect) of the given phenomenon.

As we shall see the Method of Agreement is a method of finding that a given factor is a necessary condition. Essentially it depends on finding many instances of the effect, that is, many *positive instances* which show the greatest possible negative analogy. Thereby the positive analogy is reduced. In the positive analogy there must be the *essential* positive analogy, or necessary condition. Using the Method of Agreement, the number of factors which can be necessary conditions is restricted.

We consider a number of positive instances, that is, instances which all contain the effect E which are otherwise as unalike as possible. A large number of such instances may be observed by the scientist, but, for obvious reasons we will take a small number for our example. Let us say that the different factors in the instances are represented by capital letters. Then among the positive instances let us say there are the following factors:

1st positive instance factors			PQRS
2nd ,,	,,	,,	PQST
3rd ,,	,,	,,	PRUV
4th ,,	,,	,,	PRSU

It will be observed that the only factor common to all the instances is P. P represents the positive analogy and the factors represented by QRSTUV are all part of the negative analogy. None of this latter group of factors can possibly contain a necessary condition for the effect. It follows that the only possible necessary conditions must be sought in P.

We may now see more clearly why increasing the negative analogy will help us to become more and more certain that the necessary conditions for E, the effect, have been found. For, as the factors represented by QRSTUV etc. are increased, the number of possible necessary conditions for E becomes less. Every increase in the negative analogy is accompanied by a corresponding decrease in the positive analogy. There is therefore a decrease in the number of factors which have to be considered as possible necessary conditions. As we saw in chapter 2, section iii, accumulating instances indiscriminately, while not entirely useless, is unlikely to give us very much knowledge about the essential positive analogy or necessary conditions. It is only if we are guided by some theory as to what factors are relevant that the Method of Argreement will have much practical use.

A theory as to necessary conditions indicates what factors might be relevant. Experiments can be planned in which these various factors are eliminated, to test whether the effect E will still occur. If the effect does still occur then some or all of the remaining factors must contain the necessary conditions, but at least some possible factors have been eliminated. The Method of Agreement is the method of collecting positive instances, with the purpose of enlarging the negative analogy and so eliminating possible necessary conditions.

But however many observations are made it is impossible that we should be left with a single factor which is the single necessary condition. As has been pointed out, necessary conditions include the normal or 'expected' background conditions. Though the Method of Agreement does eliminate factors which might possibly have been necessary conditions, it is not possible for it to indicate explicitly the *sum total* of necessary conditions. Nor does it prevent us from taking factors in the remaining positive analogy as being necessary conditions when in fact they are not necessary conditions. The Method does not help us to formulate explicitly all the necessary causes of the effect, and it can never satisfy us completely as to all the non-necessary conditions having been eliminated.

An example of finding necessary conditions is an experiment seeking the necessary conditions for the rotting of foods. Theory indicates that foods are unlikely to rot unless they are left warm, and have at some time been exposed to air. Various foods are kept in these conditions and *other factors* are varied. The air may be allowed to be humid or dry; the food may be exposed to air for a few minutes or for some length of time; other gases may be introduced into the air; many different types of food may be tested and so on. In all cases a mould grows and/or putrefaction occurs. The experiment eliminates humidity, time of exposure (within wide limits), absence of gases other than air, and variety of food as necessary conditions for rotting. It indicates that exposure to air and warmth may be necessary conditions and so confirms the original theory.

Mill himself did not appreciate the value of the Method of Agreement. This was because by *cause* Mill understood *sufficient condition*, not *necessary condition*. Now we have seen that the Method of Agreement is a method for finding possible necessary conditions by elimination. Since a necessary condition is required for the effect to be produced, the Method of Agreement is also a method for finding an effect which requires the cause, that is, what has been described as an effect sufficient for the cause. For, using the Method of Agreement, the effect E has been invariably observed and the necessary condition must have preceded it. But we must agree with Mill, that as method for finding sufficient conditions (or as Mill would say, *causes*) the Method of Agreement is not very satisfactory. We may see that the experiments or observations represented by the letters R S T U etc. do not indicate in any way that these factors are not perfectly good *sufficient* conditions, for the effect, E has been shown to follow after all of them. All that the experiments and/or observations have done so far as discovering sufficient conditions is concerned is to *show* that P, could be a sufficient condition as well as a possible necessary condition.

Taking the example, to find the necessary conditions for rotting of food: the experiments do not indicate that keeping the air humid and eliminating other gases etc. were not sufficient conditions for rotting. All we can say is that warmth and exposure to air are a little more likely to be sufficient conditions (as well as being necessary conditions) because in every test they were present.

Therefore, as a method for finding sufficient conditions, the Method of Agreement is a method based on induction by enumeration, it is not a method based on elimination. This type of induction is unreliable for it is not a method of testing a hypothesis by making any attempt to look for negative instances. Bacon quotes the case of the memorial tablet erected to thank God for saving those who had been in peril at sea. The list of names was long, but where, asks Bacon, is the list of those who were drowned? Quite rightly Mill said that the Method of Agreement was not a reliable method for finding causes, because he had sufficient conditions in mind.

However, Mill's second Method, the Method of Difference, *is* a method for finding sufficient conditions by elimination. The Method is described by Mill as follows:

> If an instance in which the phenomenon under investigation occurs, and an instance in which it does not occur, have every circumstance in common save one, that one occurring only in the former; the circumstance in which alone the two instances differ is the effect, or the cause, or an indispensable part of the cause, of the phenomenon.

The comment made prior to the statement of the Method of Agreement applies here, namely that Mill assumed what are in fact impossible conditions. Circumstances cannot differ in one respect only, so that otherwise two instances are the same. It is because of the practical difficulties resulting from the impossibility of this condition that more than two instances must be taken. We take one positive instance, and compare it with negative instances which are as like it as possible, save that they are negative instances. Thus we might have:

Positive instance contains factors PQRS
1st negative instance contains factors QRST
2nd   ,,   ,,   ,,   ,,   RSTU
3rd   ,,   ,,   ,,   ,,   QRSU
4th   ,,   ,,   ,,   ,,   QSUT

It is clear that any factor which appears in a negative instance cannot be a sufficient condition of the effect E. By the Method of Difference we therefore eliminate possible sufficient conditions. In the above example the only possible sufficient condition must be amongst the factors represented by P. It must be emphasised that a theory must guide us in selecting what factors we shall eliminate to obtain negative instances. In other words it is theory which suggests that certain factors P may be relevant.

It may be pointed out that the Method of Difference is not a good method for finding necessary conditions. Each of the remaining factors in the positive instance, that is, Q R S, though they have been eliminated as sufficient conditions, might yet be necessary for the effect, though not sufficient in themselves. Moreover, though the Method of Difference has indeed confirmed that P *could* be necessary, as well as sufficient, it provides us with no evidence on which to base a choice of P rather than Q R or S as a necessary condition.

An example of the application of the Method of Difference to finding a sufficient condition is the investigation of the effect of smoking on lung cancer. A hypothesis based on knowledge that tar from tobacco contains carcinogens leads us to test whether smokers are more likely to suffer from lung cancer. Our positive instance must consist of a group of smokers. We are going to compare the percentage incidence of lung cancer among members of the group with the incidence among other groups *which are as like the first group as possible* except that the members are not smokers. It is found that the incidence of lung cancer among members of the group is higher than its incidence among similar groups of the same age, sex, and place of dwelling. The evidence indicates that smoking is a sufficient cause of lung cancer in so far as smokers have a given percentage incidence of lung cancer which is higher than the percentage for non-smokers. It may be objected that a similar experiment could reveal that town dwellers were more likely to suffer from lung cancer than were country dwellers, but this had been allowed for in the experiment, in that the non-smokers compared with the smokers were from the same type of dwelling place. The objection does, however, show how important it is that all relevant factors, apart from the factor under test, be kept the same in the two groups. Only knowledge of the situation and hypotheses of relevance based on that knowledge, can indicate what factors are or might be relevant. Errors arise when a factor dismissed as irrelevant, and therefore not carefully controlled in each group, is in fact relevant.

If we are comparing town dwellers with country dwellers we may find that town dwelling is *also* a sufficient condition for lung cancer, in that the percentage incidence amongst town dwellers is higher than that for country dwellers. An effect may well have more than one sufficient condition. But this does not undermine the evidence provided by the observations comparing smokers with non-smokers, *provided that* the two groups were similarly situated as regarded their dwelling.

A necessary and sufficient condition may be found by application of the Joint Method of Agreement and Difference. This was stated by Mill as follows:

> If two or more instances in which the phenomenon occurs have only one circumstance in common, while two or more instances in which it does not occur have nothing in common save the absence of that circumstance, the circumstance in which alone the two sets of instances differ is the effect, or the cause, or an indispensable part of the cause of the phenomenon.

Again we should note that Mill requires conditions of similarity and difference which are impossible to achieve in practice. It is essential to have some hypothesis as to cause in order to apply the Method. The Method should be reworded to state that instances have only one *relevant* circumstance in common, and only one *relevant* circumstance by which they differ.

We may take the example of Semmelweiss's investigation to illustrate the Method. Semmelweiss knew that among the factors present in the First Division cases there must be something which was a necessary condition and something which was a sufficient condition for the higher death rate. His clue was that at least the sufficient condition must be a factor which was not present among the Second Division cases. He altered those factors operating in the First Division which he knew to be different from the Second Division. His first experiments on the mode of the priest's arrival, the position of delivery etc., were all shown to be irrelevant. Therefore they could not be necessary conditions for the higher death rate, for this high death rate occurred whether the factors were operating or not. Finally he was guided by the death of his friend to the hypothesis that the coming of the medical students direct from the dissecting rooms with contaminated hands was a necessary condition for the high death rate. His positive instances had all contained this factor. That was the circumstance common to all his positive instances though other relevant conditions had been varied. However, Semmelweiss then continued to show that the necessary condition was also a sufficient condition. This was done by showing that *after* the medical students were required to wash their hands in chloride of lime, the death rate was lowered. This was the only relevant change in the circumstances. Thus the Method of Agreement showed that the condition was a necessary condition and the Method of Difference showed that it was a sufficient condition; Semmelweiss had applied the Joint Method.

Mill proposed two more Methods: the Method of Residues and the Method of Concomitant Variations. The Method of Residues states that if known causes cannot account for an effect then it is necessary to seek a cause elsewhere, that is, there must be some residual factor which is not known and/or has not been taken into account. A famous example of the application of the Method is the investigations leading to the discovery of the planet since called Neptune, which was the 'residual cause' that produced the effect of disturbing the motion of the planet Uranus. This has been described in chapter 6, section iv. It was known that the perturbations in the orbit of Uranus were not due to the gravitational pull of the other known planets, and, if Newton's theory of gravitational attraction were correct, there must be some body exerting a force on Uranus. However, this conclusion was not arrived at by a process of induction, it was a consequence of deductive reasoning. Similarly the detailed calculations whereby the orbit of the unknown planet was determined were examples of deductive and mathematical reasoning, not of inductive inference. The initial hypothesis, in this case that the disturbance was due to another unknown planet, *may* be arrived at by some form of unconscious induction, but no Methods are available to describe that. Apart from the possibility of this unconscious induction, there is no induction in the Method of Residues.

The Method of Concomitant Variations was stated by Mill as:

> Whatever phenomenon varies in any manner whenever another phenomenon varies in some particular manner, is either a cause or an effect of that phenomenon, or is connected with it through some fact of causation.

Mill said that this Method was applicable when a given factor could not be removed, but could only be reduced, so that the Method of Difference was not applicable. Hypothesis might suggest that it was essential, but this could not be proved by observation, that is, by seeing the effect of removing it. An example of the Method of Concomitant Variations is the investigation of the effect of pressure on the volume of a gas kept at constant temperature. The pressure cannot be reduced to zero, so that the Method of Difference cannot be applied. But since observation shows us that alternation of pressure can cause a corresponding inverse alteration of volume, we can take it that there is some causal relation between them.

It has been shown that Mill's Methods are essentially methods designed to test hypotheses as to cause, and that, like all empirical tests, they are best applied as methods of elimination. It is also apparent that a *series* of experiments must be performed to show that a given phenomenon is a necessary and/or sufficient condition of another phenomenon. We therefore have observations based on a class of tests in which the cause C appears with the effect E, and another class of tests in which the cause C does not appear and nor does the effect E. In the series of experiments, the various Cs are similar but not identical, and the same is true of the Es. Therefore to say that C is a necessary condition of E is really to say 'If a member of the class of Es occurs then a member of the class of Cs must have occurred'. Similarly, if we say that C is a sufficient condition of E we are really saying 'If a member of the class of Cs occurs, then a member of the class of Es will occur', or 'If a member of the class of Es does not occur then a member of the class of Cs has not occurred'. It follows that we cannot justify talk about 'causal essence' as being a relation between a given cause and effect, but we can say that there is some underlying relation between the class of causes and the class of effects. This of course is because, when reformulated, the causal relation becomes a statement which is a well-attested empirical generalisation or a scientific law.

To summarise, we may say that the relation of cause and effect represents just one way of describing events in the empirical world. It can be misleading in that we may be tempted to regard causes as being the result of the action of conscious agents with a given end, the effect, in view. If we wish to emphasise the temporal relation, we should regard the causal relation as being a description of a process, the cause being the start of the process and the effect the end of the process in the particular system under consideration. But we need not insist on a temporal aspect, for causal relations can always be reformulated either as non-temporal empirical generalisations or as laws. Cause and effect do have a time order in our thoughts, but we can dispense with this. If we understand how causal relations can be reformulated as laws or as established empirical generalisations, we may see why it is that there is a tendency to regard cause and effect as being connected in some special way. The connection reflects the confidence there is in the truth of the generalisation or law. In the case of the law, the confidence is partly based on confidence in the scientific theory which supports the law, but, at the last, trust in law and theory depends on the results of observation. It is regular and invariable association which gives us confidence. Our animal faith in inductive inference leads us to rely on causal relation, and the fact that we have this faith is shown by our confidence in causal relations. Causal relations and laws of nature are but different ways of describing and predicting events in the empirical world. (See p. 141 for Questions and Further Reading related to this chapter.)

8

Probability

(i) Two Probability Problems

The casual use of 'probable' in everyday speech, for example, 'Probably it will be fine tomorrow' is taken to mean 'More likely than not, I think, it will be fine tomorrow'. If challenged as to why I think this is so, I might have to admit that it was no more than a hope. On the other hand I might be able to produce evidence 'Red sky at night, shepherds' delight – and the sky tonight is red', or, perhaps less reliable, the radio weather report.

An assertion of probability which is based on observation (our own and/or that of others) is the only type with which we are concerned in empirical science. All the synthetic propositions of science are established by reference to experience, and this means that they are at least tested, if not arrived at, by processes which involve induction. No proposition which is supported by induction can be regarded as indubitable. This is not only because inductive inference itself cannot have validity analogous to that of deductive inference – this aspect can be set aside as irrelevant when we are considering the practice of the empirical scientist. It is rather because we can never be quite sure that we have discovered the essential positive analogy on which our empirical laws are based, and therefore we can never be quite sure that these laws will not need to be altered or qualified. Hence we cannot say that empirical generalisations, laws and theories are indubitable; we can only say that they show a certain degree of probability of being true. The confidence we have in the soundness of any inductive argument is, at the last, dependent on judgement, and usually on experience of the particular topic. The more technical the proposition, the more necessary will it be to have special knowledge in order even to be in a position to try to assess the reliability, or probability, of the proposition being true.

There is also another aspect of probability in relation to empirical generalisations and laws. Very many empirical generalisations and laws are not universal propositions of the type of Boyle's law or Ohm's law; they are statistical generalisations. They do not assert that 'All A is B' or 'No A is B'; they assert that 'X per cent of As are Bs'. Semmelweiss observed that the percentage of cases of death from puerperal fever in his First Division was markedly higher than the percentage of deaths in his Second Division. This was a comparison of two empirical generalisations both of which were statistical generalisations. Similarly we use statistical generalisations when we say that the percentage of cases of death from lung cancer is higher among a group of smokers than among an otherwise similar group of non-smokers. However, if we considered a particular individual in the First Division, or a particular smoker, we could not make a firm prediction as to whether she would or would not die of puerperal fever, or whether he or she would or would not die of lung cancer.

But unlike the assessment of the probability of the generalisation (universal or statistical) being true, the probability of the outcome of a particular event which is related to the statistical generalisation can be given a numerical value.* It is the convention to give probability values from zero to one. If we say that the probability of an event occurring is *one*, we are asserting that we think it will certainly occur. If we say that the probability is zero, we are asserting that we think it will certainly not occur. Intermediate values of probability indicate our confidence, or lack of confidence, in relation to the particular event. Thus when Semmelweiss found the death rate from puerperal fever in the First Division was 11.4 per cent in 1846, it *could* be said that the probability of any particular patient dying from puerperal fever in that year was .114. The probability of a patient in the Second Division dying was only between .02 and .03. (See this chapter, section iv.)

We should bear in mind that numerical probabilities which are derived from statistical generalisations arrived at by observation should be distinguished from what are known as mathematical or *a priori* probabilities. If we say that the probability of an evenly weighted coin coming down 'heads' is .5, we judge this to be the probability, not because we have tossed many different coins, many times

---

* If the event is related to a universal generalisation, its probability must be either one or zero.

each and have found that 'heads' appeared in half the number of times, but from considerations of symmetry. Similarly we may calculate the probability of throwing a series of say ten 'heads'. This would in fact be $1/_2 10 = .0009765$, and the probability of throwing a series of 100 'heads' would be $1/_2 100$ which is approximately .0000000000000000000000000000013. The longer the series of 'heads', the lower is the probability that they will be tossed, but it will never be zero. There is always a chance, though an ever smaller chance as the number in question is greater, that in any finite series a coin will fall 'heads' each time.

But if we assume an infinite number of throws this is not the case. Consideration that one is half of two makes it certain that there will be an equal number of 'heads' and 'tails' for the ideal coin. The limiting frequency of 'heads' is .5. To say that there is a limiting frequency of .5 is to say that the frequency of 'heads' will be $.5 \pm \varepsilon$ where ε is a number as small as we choose. The greater the number of throws, the smaller ε can be. Thus, in the long run, we shall be very close to the limiting frequency $- .5$ in this case. It might be said, following Keynes, that in the long run we are all dead and therefore the concept of limiting frequency is of no great concern. But this is not the case. Given any finite number of throws it is possible to calculate the *probability* of nearness to approach to the limiting frequency *a priori*; and the probability is very high that we shall be close to the limiting frequency even in a relatively short run of throws. The probability of any given 'spread' from .5 can be calculated. Of course a highly improbable frequency of 1 for 'heads' on 100 throws cannot be absolutely ruled out – this is the starting point of the Stoppard play *Rosencrantz and Guildenstern are Dead*, but in that play it is rightly regarded as a fantasy. We assume that the highly improbable will not happen, and we act as though it will be impossible.

Now, if we are given an actual coin we may well use the mathematical *a priori* probability to predict how it will fall. For instance we could say that on ten successive throws it would be very unlikely to fall 'heads' every time, and that it would be most likely that there would be five 'heads' and five 'tails'. Usually the results of such predictions agree 'pretty nearly' but we must remember that *a priori* probabilities are based on ideal coins, absolutely evenly weighted and absolutely fairly tossed, and no object or event in the world is quite like the ideal. Therefore, although *a priori* probability may be an invaluable guide, we are finally dependent on observation and experience for establishing probabilities of events.

But the notion of limiting frequency can also be applied to actual empirical events as well as to *a priori* mathematical idealisations. Given an actual coin we might start, guided by *a priori* mathematics, by assuming that the limiting frequency of 'heads' would be .5. But after a certain number of throws we might find that there were slightly more 'heads' than 'tails' and we might come to the conclusion, based on empirical evidence, (that is, observation) that the limiting frequency of 'heads' was .502. The fact that we take it that there *is* a limiting frequency is based on the assumption that inductive reasoning is reliable. This is the assumption that Reichenbach (see chapter 4, section viii) says we must make if we are to learn anything about the world and if we are to make any empirical predictions. However, though we may assume that there is a limiting frequency, it is not possible to arrive at an indubitable value for that frequency because we cannot make an infinite number of throws. Hence, after a finite number of throws, we must be content to suggest that there is a certain probability of a limiting frequency of a certain value. This probability can be calculated mathematically, and the greater the number of throws the higher it will be. But the decision as to how high a probability we require, or, put in another way, how low a probability that the allotted limiting frequency is wrong, is an arbitrary one, (see also this chapter, section iii). Even in a given specific situation people may differ because the toleration allowed will depend on personal judgement. Though clearly some people will be much better qualified to assess permitted toleration in a given situation than others.

So, even if we set aside doubts as to the validity of inductive inference, we still have to consider two types of probability. First, there is the probability that the inductive generalisation itself is true, that is, the problem of the probability that no essential positive analogy has been overlooked. This is a problem for both universal and statistical generalisations. Second, there is the problem of probability in connection with the application of a statistical generalisation to a series of cases and to a particular case.

(ii) The Probability of the Truth of Generalisations, Laws and Theories

When we assess the probability that an empirical generalisation, law or theory is true we can only speak in terms of an intuitive non-numerical probability and it is arguable that the term 'probability' as applied to such generalisations is misleading.

We cannot relate their probability to *a priori* mathematical data, as we can when stating the probability that a given penny will turn up 'heads' in a series of throws. Neither can we relate the probability to the number of observations made, which have confirmed a given generalisation. There may well be a very large number of confirming instances, that is, observations which have supported the generalisation. But in relation to the indefinitely large number of possible confirming instances (past present and future), that is, observations which might have supported the generalisation but were not made, as well as those which were made, the number of actual confirming instances must be indefinitely small, and the ratio of confirmed instances to total possible instances is zero for all practical purposes. Hence a probability estimate based on this ratio would have to be zero.

We may note here an important difference *of approach* between the generalisation and a particular event when we are attempting to find out if it is helpful to speak of the probability of the generalisation being true or of the particular event occurring. If we are concerned with a single event, say whether a horse X will win a race, we seek as much evidence as we can (the past performance of the horse and that of the other horses in the race, their state of health, the skill of the jockeys etc.) and it is *felt* that some numerical value can be given to the probability of X winning. Betting odds illustrate this (though they will be weighted in favour of the bookmaker, and, in the case of the Tote they are also affected by the actual wagers made by the punters). It might be thought that these odds also illustrate how inaccurate (even allowing for weighting) such estimates can be since the actual results of a race are notoriously unrelated to the odds in a very large number of cases. But this in itself does not reflect on the reliability of the probability estimate. For, if I make an estimate of the probability of a given event occurring, say of my drawing the Ace of Spades from a pack of cards, and another estimate of the probability of my drawing a red card, then my estimate of the probability of drawing the Ace of Spades would be $1/52 = .0192$ – a probability which is considerably less than the probability of drawing a red card, which is $1/2 = .5$. But neither estimate of probability is shown to be incorrect if I actually draw the Ace of Spades. No more does the fact that an 'outsider' at long odds wins a race show, in itself, that those odds were incorrect or that the odds allotted to the other horses were incorrect.

In the case of the cards the numerical probability is obtained from *a priori* considerations discussed in the previous section, whereas in the case of the horses all the evidence contributing to the probability estimate is empirical. Although it is patently obvious that numerical estimates (betting odds) are made in relation to a particular event (a horse winning a given race), I would contend that the use of the term 'probability' is just as misleading as when it is applied to generalisations. As we obtain more and more evidence we are approaching not a more accurate *probability* estimate but a firm prediction. If *all* the relevant evidence were known, and for a past event this might be possible, in principle if not in fact, we would be able to retrodict truly the position of our horse, and the position of all the other horses, at the end of the race – there would be no need to introduce the notion of probability. In the case of future events it is logically impossible to have all the information, but the nearer the future event is to the present the more likely are we to be able to have sufficient information to move from some vague and misleading assertion of probability to a definite prediction. The assertion of probability is vague because there is no accepted method for calculating the number and it is misleading because it is nearer to being a confession of lack of confidence than to being a probability estimate analogous to probability estimates derived from *a priori* considerations or from empirical statistical generalisations.

But to return to empirical generalisations, laws and theories, we have to admit that we do speak of such propositions as being probably true, or having *a probability* of being true. But this is merely a way of saying that we are going to treat the propositions as being true (and act accordingly) until such time as further observation gives us reason to alter our opinion.

(iii) *The Probability of the Truth of Statistical Generalisations*

Empirical statistical generalisations, as opposed to *a priori* statistical generalisations, are obtained by observing a selected class of instances and noting the proportion of cases where an event in which we are interested occurs. Semmelweiss obtained his statistical generalisation of deaths from puerperal fever in his First Division by noting the number of such deaths in proportion to the total number of patients in the Division. Clearly the reliability of the statistical generalisation is closely related to the number of patients. If Semmelweiss had had only 50 patients in the year the significance of his generalisation would not have been so great as if there had been 1000 patients. But there are other factors which affect the reliability and significance of statistical generalisations, and this indeed has led to the epigram 'There are liars, damn liars and statisticians'. In the Semmelweiss example the problem of which cases were to be considered was a simple one, but this is not generally so. In most circumstances it is necessary to take a somewhat arbitrary decision as to what cases are to be examined. For example, suppose we are to make an estimate of the proportion of brown hens' eggs, and therefore the probability that we shall have a brown egg for breakfast, do we consider all the eggs laid by hens in England, or the eggs laid by a certain breed of hen, or the eggs laid by hens in our area, or on a given diet, or obtained from a certain battery farm etc.?

But let us assume that we have decided on a class, that we have made a satisfactory number of observations and that we have arrived at a statistical generalisation that ten per cent of the eggs are brown. We might say that the probability of having a brown egg for breakfast was .1. Now how do we test the truth of the generalisation or of the probability statement? In the case of a universal generalisation tests can be designed to attempt to refute. As we have seen (chapter 6, section i), refutation may not be a simple matter but it is even less simple with a statistical generalisation. For though in the case say of hens' eggs we expect one egg in ten to be brown we cannot definitely affirm that the generalisation and the probability estimate are false if, in a sample of ten eggs, there were no brown ones, or even if they were all brown. Of course if we took 1000 eggs and found all were brown (or none were brown) our confidence in the statistical generalisation would be shaken. But *how many* eggs need to be examined?

We claim that the probability that the proportion of positive instances (such as brown eggs) in a new series will be the same as the proportion established by a previous series of observations – this is a second-order probability – will be 1, if we are confident of the truth of our original statistical generalisation. It must be stressed that if the proportion in the new series is not exactly the same as the proportion previously established this will not necessarily affect our second-order probability estimate of 1, for we must expect a small 'spread'.

But we will tolerate only a small 'spread'. If the new proportion differs greatly we take it that the original empirical statistical generalisation has been refuted. It might not have been, especially if the new series were small (see above), but we regard the occurrence of a proportion which is markedly different from a proportion previously established as giving evidence which undermines the truth of the previous generalisation. But again, *how different* must the proportion be? How big a 'spread' will we accept?

Statistical generalisations are found in great numbers in the social sciences and in medicine where there are so many factors which must be taken into account and which cannot be controlled in anything like the same way that they can be controlled in the physical sciences. The statistical generalisations reflect these limitations and our consequent lack of knowledge. They cannot be as useful as universal generalisations: they can be the basis for a probability prediction in regard to an individual but even then the use is limited because the assumption is that the individual is randomly selected and that nothing else is known about him except that he is a member of the class considered. In practice this is not generally the case and the crude probability prediction can be highly misleading. For example, it has been said that the probability of a patient dying of puerperal fever in Semmelweiss's First Division in 1846 would be .114, but if the age of the patient and her general health, to name but two factors, were taken into account, that crude probability figure would be likely to be misleading. The other great disadvantage of statistical generalisations is the difficulty in establishing their truth or falsehood. As has been indicated, arbitrary decisions have to be made about numbers of instances and about 'spread'.

(iv) Summary

We have to concede that all empirical generalisations, laws and scientific theories, that is, all those propositions which are supported by induction, cannot be held to be indubitable. This is not only due to doubts about the reliability of inductive inference – for practising scientists such doubts can be dismissed. But scientists must still accept that there is always a possibility that some essential positive analogy has been overlooked.

One way we indicate this uncertainty is by saying that the empirical generalisations etc. are probably true; it may be very probably true. But the qualification merely reminds us that synthetic propositions do not have the certainty of analytic propositions. *And that is all.* There is no way of assessing this 'probability' numerically and since there are numerical probabilities which can be allotted to certain types of events and series of events, for example those which can be linked to *a priori* probabilities, there is ground for suggesting that the use of the term 'probability' in relation to generalisations is misleading and should be avoided.

But the notion of probability is useful if we are considering empirical statistical generalisations. In that context it can have a use *provided* (and the difficulties have been considered in the previous section ii) the generalisation is well-founded. Even so we must be careful, for if the statistics are held to be well-founded so that the generalisation is taken as being true, it is customary to say that the probability of its truth is high. Such a probability, that is, the probability of the statistical generalisation (itself indicating a probability) is as we have seen called a 'second-order' probability. Hence a statistical generalisation regarded as well-founded may be said to have a second-order probability of 1 or close to 1. As I have explained in the previous paragraph (and in section i) the use of the term 'probability' as applied to the truth of generalisations (universal or statistical) can be misleading. What we really intend when we say that the second-order probability is close to 1 (or to be taken as 1) is that we are making a decision to accept that a certain proportion of the events in a chosen series will be of a certain type. We therefore decide that we can make true predictions about a series of events and act accordingly.

There are occasions when it can be helpful to talk about the probability of the occurrence of one particular event in the series, by relating it to the probability indicated by the statistical generalisation. But it is clear that we cannot make a firm prediction about whether the event will or will not occur. Moreover there is the added uncertainty that the probability indicated may itself be unreliable, *as applied to that particular event*, because we may have to take into account factors relating to it which alter the assessment indicated by the crude over-all probability of the generalisation.

Predictions in regard to particular events which can be related to universal generalisations do not suffer from these two defects and that is why the universal generalisation is the ideal of science. (See p. 142 for Questions and Further Reading related to this chapter.)

Questions and Further Reading

1. The Nature of Induction

QUESTION

Give an example of an inductive generalisation which has come to be revised in the light of further experience. What experience(s) led to the revision?

FURTHER READING

R. L. Gregory, *The Intelligent Eye* (Weidenfeld & Nicolson, London: 1970), ch. 1.

D. W. Hamlyn, *The Psychology of Perception* (Routledge, London: 1961).

G. B. Keene, *Language and Reasoning* (Van Nostrand, London: 1961).

E. Nagel and J. R. Newman, *Gödel's Proof* (Routledge, London: 1959).

L. S. Stebbing, *A Modern Introduction to Logic* (Methuen & Co., London: 1942), chs 12 and 13.

J. H. Randall Jr, *Aristotle* (Columbia University Press, London and New York: 1962), ch. 3, sect. 1.

2. Analogy

QUESTIONS

1. Discuss the nature of analogies and show, with examples, how an

analogy may be relevant and important in one context, and irrelevant and unimportant in another context.

2. Explain with examples how it is that inductive arguments must involve analogy, and that analogical arguments must involve induction.

3. What is meant by the terms 'positive analogy' and 'negative analogy'? Give examples.

4. Why is an inductive argument strengthened most by instances which are known to increase the negative analogy between instances?

FURTHER READING

M. B. Hesse, *Models and Analogies in Science* (Notre Dame U.P., Indiana: 1962).

J. M. Keynes, *A Treatise on Probability* (Macmillan; London: 1921), ch. XVIII.

L. S. Stebbing, *A Modern Introduction to Logic* (see 1 above), ch. 14.

3. Observation and Experiment

QUESTIONS

1. What is the distinction between critical observation and experimentation? Name two sciences in which critical observation plays a more important part than experimentation, and explain why this is so.

2. Describe an example of a scientific investigation which involved active experimentation.

3. Discuss the part played by chance in a particular scientific discovery.

4. Why is it that theories are of such importance in guiding experimentation? Give an example to illustrate your answer.

5. Discuss the part played by testimony in any three chosen experimental investigations.

6. Why is weight taken as a measurable quantity whereas it is arguable whether IQ is such a quantity?

FURTHER READING

J. Black, *Experiments upon Magnesia Alba* (Alembic Club Reprint, No. 1, Livingstone, Edinburgh).

R. Carnap, ed. M. Gardner, *An Introduction to the Philosophy of Science* (Basic Books Inc., New York: 1966), Part II, chs 5–12.

C. H. Hempel *The Philosophy of Natural Science* (Prentice-Hall, Englewood Cliffs, N.J: 1966).

A. Koestler, *The Sleepwalkers* (Hutchinson, London: 1968).

P. B. Medawar, *Induction and Intuition in Scientific Thought* (Methuen, London: 1969).

J. Priestley, *The Discovery of Oxygen* (Alembic Club Reprint, No. 7, Livingstone, Edinburgh: 1961).

4. The Justification of Inductive Inference

QUESTIONS

1. What is a tautology? Give examples. Explain why the term is relative in that a tautology for one individual may not be so for another.
2. Why is it that the true mathematical propositions are analytic statements? Give some examples of logical propositions which are analytic statements. Why is it that these statements tell us nothing about the empirical world?
3. Explain clearly the nature of Hume's problem, and discuss the adequacy of Reichenbach's solution.
4. How is it that Mill and Keynes did not give an adequate answer to Hume's problem?
5. What assumption lies behind Broad's attempted solution of Hume's problem?
6. Critically discuss Popper's account of induction.
7. What is the new riddle of induction? Do you think it sensible?

FURTHER READING

A. J. Ayer, *The Origins of Pragmatism* (Macmillan, London: 1968; paperback 1974), ch. 3, sect. B.

C. D. Broad, 'The Relation between Induction and Probability', in *Induction, Probability and Causation: Selected Papers* (Reidel, Dordrecht: 1968).

N. Goodman, *Fact, Fiction and Forecast*, 3rd edn (The Bobbs-Merril Co. Inc., New York: 1973) ch. 3.

H. P. Grice and P. F. Strawson, 'In Defence of a Dogma', *The Philosophical Review*, 65 (1956), pp. 142–158.

D. Hume, *Enquiries Concerning the Human Understanding and Concerning the Principles of Morals*, edited by L. A. Selby-Bigge (Clarendon Press, Oxford; 1894; 2nd edn 1902), reprint 1970, Book I, especially sect. iv, paras 20–33 (pp. 25–40).

J. M. Keynes, *A Treatise on Probability* (see 2 above), ch. XXII.

K. Lambert and G. Brittan, *An Introduction to the Philosophy of Science* (Prentice-Hall Inc., Englewood Cliffs, N. J.: 1970), ch. 2.

J. S. Mill, *A System of Logic* 10th edn (Longmans, London: 1972), Book III, ch. 5, esp. sect. I.

K. Popper, *The Logic of Scientific Discovery* (Hutchinson, London: 1972), ch. I.

K. Popper, *Conjectures and Refutations* (Routledge, London: 1963), Introduction and ch. I.

W. V. O. Quine, 'Two Dogmas of Empiricism', in *From a Logical Point of View* (Harvard U.P., 2nd rev. edn, 1961).

B. Russell, *The Problems of Philosophy* (Oxford University Press, Oxford: 1974), chs 6 and 7.

W. C. Salmon, *The Foundations of Scientific Inference* (Pittsburgh UP, Pittsburgh: 1967).

B. Skyrms, *Choice and Chance* (Dickenson, Belmont (Cal.): 1966).

L. S. Stebbing, *A Modern Introduction to Logic* (see 1 above), ch. 21.

5.   Theories and Laws

QUESTIONS

1. What is the essential difference between hypotheses which are in the form of explanatory theories and those which are in the form of empirical generalisations? Give two examples of each.

2. How can a theory be a scientific theory even though the entities which it educes cannot be directly observed?

3. Why is it that a metaphysical theory may be helpful to the scientist?

4. Distinguish between scientific empirical generalisations and scientific laws, and give three examples of each.

5. Discuss the merits of regarding scientific theories as true descriptions of the world.

FURTHER READING

A. J. Ayer, *The Concept of a Person and Other Essays* (Macmillan, London: 1963; paperback 1973), sect. 8.

N. R. Campbell, *The Foundations of Science* (Dover, New York: 1957), ch. 2.

L. Laudan 'Progress and its Problems' (Routledge & Kegan Paul, London: 1977).

G. Maxwell, 'The Ontological Status of Theoretical Entities', in Feigl and Maxwell (eds), *Minnesota Studies in the Philosophy of Science*, vol. III (University of Minnesota Press, Minneapolis, 1962).

G. Maxwell, 'Theories, Perception and Structural Realism', in R. G. Colodny (ed.), *The Nature and Function of Scientific Theories* (Pittsburgh UP, Pittsburgh).

E. Nagel, *The Structure of Science* (Routledge, London: 1968), chs 4, 5 and 6.

F. S. C. Northrop, *The Logic of the Sciences and the Humanities* (Macmillan Publishing Co., New York: 1949), ch. 4.

K. Popper, *Conjectures and Refutations* (see 4 above), ch. 3.

L. S. Stebbing, *A Modern Introduction to Logic* (see 1 above), ch. 20.

6.   *The Refutation of Laws and Theories*

QUESTIONS

1. Explain how it is that a synthetic proposition may become a definition. Give three examples of propositions which might be regarded as empirical generalisations or as definitions.

2. Why is it that one well attested observation might refute a law, whereas an indefinitely large number of observations could never conclusively confirm it?

3. Why is it difficult to refute an established theory even with well attested observations?

FURTHER READING

R. B. Braithwaite, *Scientific Explanation* (Cambridge UP, Cambridge: 1955), ch. 1.

J. M. Copi, *Introduction to Logic* (Macmillan Publishing Co. Inc., New

York: 1972), ch. 8, sects 3 and 6.
N. R. Hanson, *Patterns of Discovery* (Cambridge UP, Cambridge: 1965).
C. G. Hempel, *Aspects of Scientific Explanation* (Free Press, New York: 1965), ch. 1.
A. Pap, *The 'A Priori' in Physical Theory* (Russell, New York: 1968).
K. Popper, *The Logic of Scientific Discovery* (see 4 above), ch. 4.
K. Popper, *Conjectures and Refutations* (see 4 above), ch. 1.

7.   *The Relation of Cause and Effect*

QUESTIONS

1. Distinguish between necessary and sufficient conditions, and give three examples of each in situations you care to choose.
2. Describe how causal relations may be reformulated as laws. Why does this remove the temporal relation between cause and effect?
3. Describe and criticise the assumptions underlying Mill's Canons of induction.

FURTHER READING

R. Carnap, *An Introduction to the Philosophy of Science* (see 3 above), Part IV, chs 19–21.
N. R. Campbell, *The Foundations of Science* (see 5 above), ch. 3.
D. Hume, ed. L. A. Selby-Bigge, *A Treatise of Human Nature* (Clarendon Press, Oxford: 1888; reprint 1973), Book I, Part III, especially sects XII–XV (pp. 130–73).
E. Meyerson, trans. K. Lowenberg *Identity and Reality* (Allen & Unwin, London: 1964), ch. 1.
J. S. Mill, *A System of Logic* (see 4 above), Book III, ch. 8.
L. S. Stebbing, *A Modern Introduction to Logic* (see 1 above), chs 17 and 18.
J. O. Wisdom, *Foundations of Inference in Natural Science* (Methuen, London: 1952), chs 11 and 19.
G. H. von Wright, *The Logical Problems of Induction* (Blackwell, Oxford: 1957), ch. 4.

8.   *Probability*

QUESTIONS

1. Why is it misleading to talk of the probability of a law or theory?
2. Give three examples of statistical generalisations. Why is it more difficult to refute a statistical generalisation than a universal generalisation?
3. Describe the ways in which statistics can be misleading.
4. Why do scientists seek universal generalisations rather than statistical generalisations?

FURTHER READING

A. J. Ayer, *The Concept of a Person . . .* (see 5 above), sect 7.
W. Kneale, *Probability and Induction* (Oxford University Press, Oxford: 1952).
K. Popper, *The Logic of Scientific Discovery* (see 4 above), ch. 10.
J. O. Wisdom, *Foundations of Inference in Natural Science* (see 7 above), chs 20 and 21.
G. H. von Wright, *The Logical Problems of Induction* (see 7 above), chs 7, 9 and 10.

Index